A 1958 aerial photograph showing the southern part of the area studied. It was taken from somewhere above Kettlewell looking south towards the railway line that runs across the top of the picture. Boundary Road, the original boundary between Horsell and Woking parishes, runs across the middle of the picture – and there is a crossroads with Chobham Road at the vertex of the 'V' formed by the intersection of Church Path and Chobham Road. Just below Boundary Road the Basingstoke Canal also runs across the middle of the picture. Bottom right are the Victorian houses facing onto Broomhall Road. Bottom left is Ferndale Road with houses facing onto the Wheatsheaf Recreation ground; behind them is the Grove. The allotments on what is, at the time of writing, the Brewery Road carpark can clearly be seen on the right of the picture just below the canal. To their left is the site of the future Kingswood Court; to their right is the edge of The Wharf. Between the Kingswood Court site and Broomhall Road stands Alwyne House with what looks like a tennis court on its eastern side; what had been the stables are to the north of the house, positioned at an angle to Broomhall Road.

6270

Eastern Horsell's development after the coming of the railway

John Craig

Woking History Society

2006

Published by
Woking History Society
The Lightbox, One Crown Square, Woking, Surrey, England. GU21 6HR

ISBN 0 9502675 3 8

Printed in the UK by
Arrow Press, 11 Riverside Park, Industrial Estate, Farnham, Surrey GU9 7UG

Contents

List of Figures

List of Tables

Acknowledgments

Naturally I am much indebted to those who have written books about Woking's history. When I arrived in Horsell some 35 years ago an early purchase was J R and S E Whiteman's *Victorian Woking*. Next came Alan Crosby's book which, fortunately for me, he recently updated and extended. Then there are several books and other publications by Iain Wakeford. These all gave relevant background and direct leads to this study of a small part of Horsell.

When I started to look at my small corner I would not have got very far had I not had the convenience of the Surrey History Centre, with its wonderful sets of records, being in Woking. The staff there have been unfailingly helpful much beyond the call of duty. It was also my good fortune that the Centre held a series of talks on the sources of information for local historians at just the right time – when I had started to get going on my topic but before I had spent much time on the less obvious sources.

Then several individuals with Horsell connections helped with information or by passing me onto an acquaintance who could help. These include Ann Harington, Phillip Arnold, Richard Christophers, Mrs Parfitt, David Enticknap, Kate Lloyd-Hitt, Major Holden, Ray Banks; apologies to anyone whose name I have forgotten. At a more official level I had queries willingly answered by Dorian Leveque of the British Library (Oriental and India Office Collections), Brian Yorke of the BFSS Archive Centre (Brunel University), and Sally Elder of Woking Borough Council. Photographs were provided by Mrs Parfitt (Figure 8), Bill Lindop (Figure 12), and Vera Namsoo (Figures 13(a) and 13(b)). Ann Harington provided me with a copy of the 1924 map (Figure 1 and front cover). Figures 2, 6, 7(a) & (b), 9(a) & (b), 11(a) & (b) and Appendix 1 are from the Surrey History Centre's collections and are reproduced by permission of the Surrey History Service. The aerial photograph used as the frontispiece is also from the Surrey History Centre's collections and is reproduced by kind permission of Aerofilms Limited. The map extract used on the front cover and in Figure 1 is reproduced with the permission of Eltons The Stationers.

Alfred Vice commented on an early version of this paper and Jan Mihell gave it a final polish. My wife has done her best to improve my literary style – as well as being tolerant over this impediment to my being more useful about the house. But I have had the last word; what has been written and what has not been written is wholly my decision.

I am grateful to the Woking History Society for agreeing to publish the booklet; in particular to Jan Mihell for her advice regarding the publication arrangements.

Preface

This study began with an interest in the history of my Victorian house; this soon expanded into the history of adjoining houses and then the surrounding area. This area happens to be the part of Horsell parish that is nearest to Woking Station. The railway opened in 1838 so what subsequently happened can be traced using the population censuses from 1841 onwards. The outcome is an account of how a remote, rural, and largely uninhabited part of Surrey changed during Queen Victoria's reign and, in less detail, thereafter.

The booklet contains what I have been able to find out. It has limitations as a historical study for I have not attempted to make it part of a bigger picture. For example I have not unravelled the causes of the changes that took place – how much were changes in Victorian society as a whole and how much they resulted from more local influences. Nor have I been able to pin down the differences in land ownership, which affected how developments occurred. On the other hand by concentrating on a small area it is possible to trace changes in individual dwellings and individual people as well as in aggregates.

The study should be of interest to those with a personal connection with the area. But I hope it has a wider appeal as another bit of grassroots evidence in how much Britain changed in Queen Victoria's reign or, if you like, in how suburban life replaced the rural one.

There are some 'housekeeping' points to be made. First, street names change over time. Generally today's names are used with a mention of the earlier name if appropriate. Second, surnames and house names are not always spelt in the same way in each census. Here the spelling as in a particular census has been retained so there may be apparent inconsistencies. Third, the terms 'waste' 'manorial waste' 'moor' and 'common' are used about the same piece of land by different writers. Here too the differences have been retained although they are usually of no great significance. Fourth, SHC is the abbreviation for Surrey History Centre; its catalogue number is given when documents in its collections are being cited.

Finally I have a strong suspicion that some readers will have personal knowledge of, or access to, information that is not recorded in the more formal sources I have used. For example there must be many old plans, photographs and maps buried away in drawers and cupboards. I will be delighted to be told of any such treasures.

John Craig
Kilifi, 23 Broomhall Road, Horsell, Surrey GU21 4AP
Tel 01483 762059   e-mail craigkilifi@aol.com

February 2006

1.   Preliminaries

1.1   The area studied

The part of Horsell parish where the effects of the coming in 1838 of the railway would be likely to appear soonest was that near the bridge which carries the road to Chobham over the Basingstoke Canal. This bridge is about 400 metres from the railway station. From 1841 to 1901 changes can be monitored from the findings of the decennial Censuses of Population. Other sources are listed in the Bibliography.

The area to be taken as being within easy reach of the canal bridge has, inevitably, arbitrary boundaries. Fortunately the original settlement pattern had a natural gap between the few dwellings in the vicinity of the bridge and the rest of Horsell. Each census enumerator entered this area at one end and left it at the other so the dwellings relevant to this study were enumerated successively if not always in exactly the same order; and their location was often not recorded. If the enumerator came along the ancient track from the north, the relevant area started near the top of the ridge at Kettlewell. From there dwellings adjoining, or near, the track – now Chobham Road – were enumerated until the canal bridge was reached. Any dwellings just over the bridge were included (the parish boundary, with Woking parish, was about 70 yards south of the canal along the line of the old Rive Ditch). The enumerator would come back over the canal and leave the area by heading west – along today's Brewery Road – towards Horsell village. Alternatively the enumerator could enter the area from the west and reverse the process. For convenience the area will be referred to as the 'Wheatsheaf area'.

Figure 1.   The area of interest as shown on a 1924 map

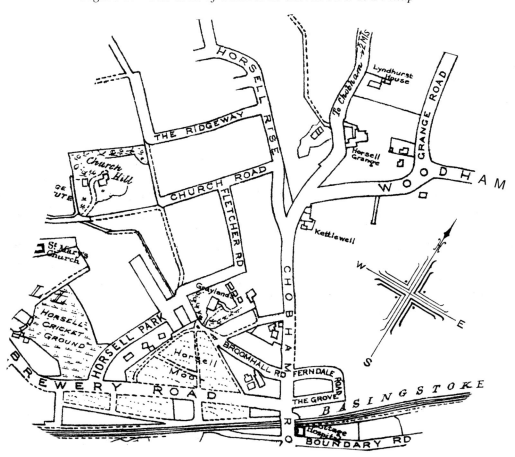

Horsell parish is the land to the north of Boundary Road. Horsell Grange is about the top of the Kettlewell ridge and is about 800 metres from the bridge over the canal. The frontispiece shows the southern end of the area and its proximity to the railway.

1.2   Before the railway

John Rocque's 1762 map of Surrey shows several dwellings at the ancient settlement of Kettlewell. This is not surprising as Kettlewell was well sited on a ridge of cultivated, better-drained, land. In contrast the lower land to the south was an uncultivated part of Woking Heath – with just one building. The same pattern is evident on the first edition Ordnance Survey one inch to the mile map of 1816 – with the addition of two or three dwellings at a place known as 'The Moor' and another near the canal to the east of the track to Kettlewell. This picture seems reliable as all these dwellings can be matched with dwellings to be found on Ryde's much more detailed 1851 map.

The railway, like the canal, had been constructed across the waste because, as it was almost worthless, the landowner was unlikely to make difficulties or require much compensation. Thus the station was built on uninhabited and uncultivated land marked on maps as Woking Heath or Woking Common – so the latter was the obvious, if unexciting, name given to the station when trains started to run in 1838. Crosby (Crosby 2003: 68) wrote 'The station was surrounded by open heathland, dotted with a few trees and a lot of gorse … That total isolation was not destined to be of long duration.' Crosby also reproduced a picture of the station and observes that, despite some artistic licence, 'the prevailing impression of an entirely rural and completely unpopulated landscape are convincing.' Another pointer to the character of the area is a report that 'When the railway was first opened the neighbourhood was so secluded that a spot in Horsell parish, near the Basingstoke Canal, was selected as a suitable place for a prize fight, as out of observation of the police.' (*Victoria County History of Surrey* 1911; 427.)

The 1841 Census gives only very broad geographical detail but fortunately there is the detailed 1851 map – Figure 2. This is copied from the map of Horsell parish prepared by Edward Ryde. (See the Bibliography.) The details are commented on later but it demonstrates the sparse and scattered nature of the dwellings in 1851 – which, as is also shown later, was not very different from 1841. In turn, most of the heads of household in the 1841 Census can be found in the 1834 Survey of Horsell Parish – indicating that there had been little, if any, development in the area in anticipation of, or immediately following, the arrival of the railway. (For technical reasons in Figure 2 it is impractical to include the whole of the area studied – it extends a little further to the north and west.)

1.3   The growth of the railway service

This is not to suggest that all the development in the area after 1838 can be attributed to the coming of the railway. Clearly this was a crucial factor but it interacted with many others. By way of background a measure of how the train service improved during the 19th Century can be given. The indicator chosen is the number of trains leaving Woking for London, both express and slow, between 6am and noon. The timetable for 1843 had just 3 departures in the six hours. The numbers for 1860, 1880, and 1900 grew from 5 to 6 and 13 respectively. Thus the service steadily improved – with the biggest improvement occurring towards the end of the century. (But even the 1900 service was nothing like today's; the comparable figure for 2005 was 72 departures). The fastest journey time in 1843 was 47 minutes (to Nine Elms); this was down to 36 minutes to Waterloo in 1900. The 1860 and 1880 timetables show that on most trains horses and carriages could be carried. By 1900 they were restricted to a special in the morning and another in the afternoon.

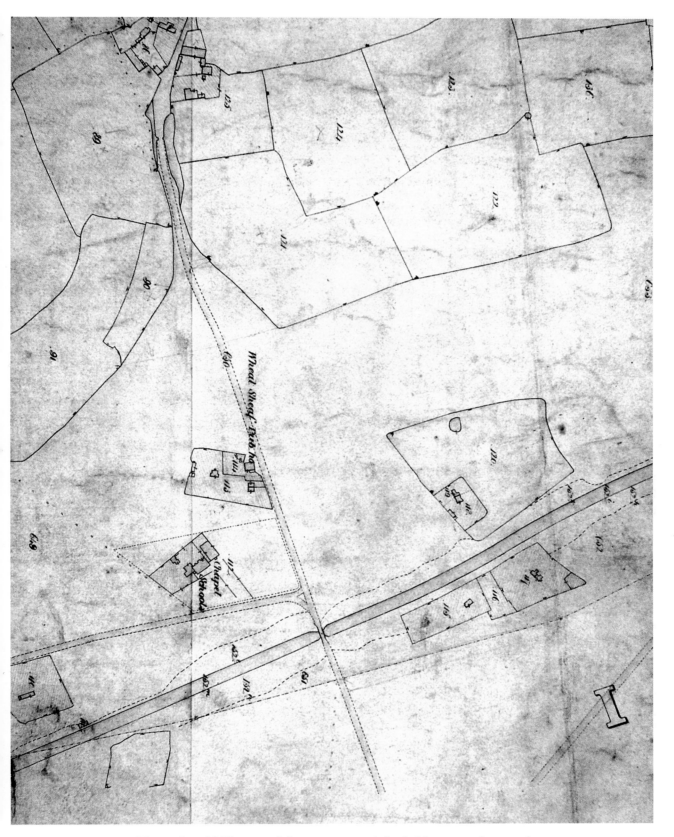

Figure 2. 1851 map of the area around the bridge over the canal

This map was not drawn so north was 'at the top'. This is achieved, approximately, by rotating the map through 90 degrees. This Figure is a slight reduction in size of the original on which 1 inch represented 200 feet; on this copy that has increased to about 280 feet. The area considered in this study extends slightly further north and west but for technical reasons it is impractical to include these areas. See Appendix 1 for the key to the plot numbers.

4

2. Population and Household Growth 1841 to 1901

2.1 An overview

Population growth of the Wheatsheaf area is compared in Figure 3 with that of the rest of Horsell parish. The two graphs are drawn in such a way that a constant rate of population growth over time would result in a straight line; and the greater the rate of growth the steeper the slope of the line. The same rates of growth, at either different times or between different areas, would have lines with the same slopes.

Figure 3. Population Growth 1841-1901

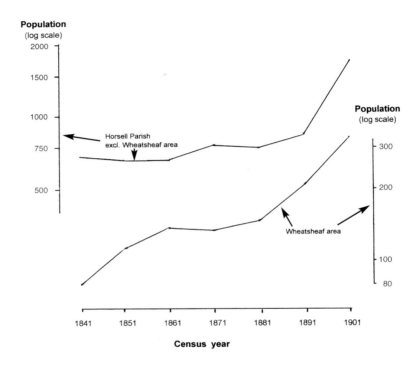

The Figure highlights that, up to 1891, the rate of growth in the Wheatsheaf area greatly exceeded that of the rest of the parish. By 1891 the population of the former was between two and three times what it had been in 1841; while the increase for the rest of the parish was only one-fifth. However from about 1891 growth in the rest of the parish took off and its population more than doubled in a decade. The population of the Wheatsheaf area did not grow quite so rapidly – even though its growth was more rapid than in any previous decade. As Crosby put it 'Horsell village remained a backwater until the 1880s' (Crosby 2003: 102) – but this was not so for the area near the canal bridge! The difference is confirmed by the author of the section on Horsell in the Victoria County History who wrote 'The aspect of the eastern part of the parish has been quite transformed by the growth of the town about Woking Junction' (VCH 1911: 427). Note the stress on the eastern part; the precise date of this comment is unknown.

Figure 3 also shows how population growth in the Wheatsheaf area varied over time. After a spurt in the first twenty years – when the population of the rest of the parish fell – there was a slowing down in 1861-71; followed by progressively larger increases in each of the three subsequent decades culminating in a 56% increase in 1891-1901. This acceleration towards the end of the century coincided with the considerable improvement in the train service.

The number of households in the area, which is closely related to – but not identical to – the number of dwellings, grew even more rapidly than the population. In 1901 there were six times as many households as in 1841 while there were just four times as many people. The divergence reflects a fall in the average household size from 6.0 to 4.3 persons per household. These large increases in population and households were accompanied by big changes in the social structure of the population.

2.2   The changing social structure

The occupations of the inhabitants of an area are often a good guide to its social structure. In each census the occupation of each individual, for whom the question was relevant, was collected. Tabulating the heads of households' occupations gives the data in Table 1. At the time of the 1841 Census, when things were probably much as they had been before the railway arrived, the area was predominantly agricultural and sparsely populated. There were just 13 households and of the 11 household heads whose occupation was recorded only three had non-agricultural occupations – none of which was railway related. It is not too surprising that the railway had had little effect for the 1841 Census was taken in the middle of a very severe economic depression when many paupers starved from lack of employment. (Wilson 2002, p28 – quoting another source.) A bricklayer's presence is the only hint of development.

Table 1.   Occupation, and Status, of Heads of Households 1841-1901

Occupation, and status, of head of household	1841	1851	1861	1871	1881	1891	1901
Higher status							
Professional	1	1	0	0	3	3	5
Business and Commerce	0	0	3	1	2	7	12
Middle status							
Public Services	1	1	2	1	1	1	4
Small businesses	0	1	2	2	1	2	14
Farmers	2	2	2	3	3	0	0
Lower status							
Artisans and similar	1	1	1	6	3	7	15
Labourers	6	10	13	10	10	13	10
of whom							
Agriculture & horticulture	*6*	*8*	*10*	*7*	*8*	*7*	*7*
Railway (incl. porters)	*0*	*2*	*3*	*2*	*1*	*1*	*1*
Bricklayers' labourers	*0*	*0*	*0*	*0*	*0*	*3*	*2*
Other	*0*	*0*	*0*	*1*	*1*	*1*	*0*
Independent & not stated	2	2	1	5	6	5	15
Total number of households	**13**	**18**	**24**	**28**	**29**	**38**	**75**
Total number of people	*79*	*112*	*136*	*132*	*151*	*206*	*322*
Persons per household	*6.1*	*6.2*	*5.7*	*4.7*	*5.2*	*5.4*	*4.3*

Source: Censuses of Population.

Notes:
1.   Retired people are included under their previous occupation if this was given.
2.   In 1851 a large residence had only a housekeeper at home. A 'professional' head of household has been imputed.
3.   'Total number of people' includes live-in servants.

By 1901 the picture was quite different. There were almost six times as many households as in 1841 so all bar one of the occupational groupings in Table 1 show big increases. The exception was that the number of household heads engaged in agriculture, or horticulture, had hardly changed. But within the 60 year period there had been sizeable variations in the trends. In the 1840s most of the increase was in labourers' households – the majority in agriculture but some in railway related jobs. These trends continued in the 1850s – together with the effects of the addition of two large gentlemen's residences. (See Section 3.1.)

After 1861 the number of labourers' households remained steady. Until 1891 high status and artisan households shared the increase in household numbers; households of middling status fell in number. Contrariwise after 1891 the biggest increase was in these middling status households; with the increase spilling over to those at the top of the lower status band and to those on the fringe of high status occupations. That bricklayers' labourers first appeared in Table 1 for 1891 is a sign of the onset of a building boom.

The category 'Independent and not stated' showed no increase in the 1840s or 1850s but trebled in the 1890s. Then the majority of these individuals were widows ranging from those living in poverty to the well off living in a large house with servants. Earlier, in 1851, the two people in this category were both recorded as 'paupers' whereas in 1841, despite the severe economic depression, there had been none. This may be a reflection of the workings of the 1834 Poor Law Act which discouraged outdoor relief; so in 1841 the unfortunate individuals would have been compelled to live in the workhouse. By the 1850s outdoor relief was again permitted.

There was no state pension in the period covered by Table 1 and therefore no official retirement age. So some people in their seventies were still working. Several heads of household who specified 'retired' also gave their previous occupation (as this gives an idea of their social status it was used in deriving Table 1).

Female heads of households were in a minority and were often in the 'Independent and not stated' occupational category. However by 1901 there were four working women – a lodging housekeeper, a milliner and two dressmakers – who were heads of household. This is another indication of the changes in the 1890s for in none of the earlier censuses had there been more than one working woman who was the head of household. In 1891 this had been a laundress, in 1881 and 1871 a schoolmistress and in 1861 and 1851 a farmer (which was probably unusual – she was a farmer's widow and had sons who may have shared the work). In 1841 there had been no female head of household.

2.3 Changes in household size and composition

The decline in the average number of persons in a household, despite the increasing number of servants in the gentlemen's residences, is shown in Table 1. This decline in household size was due to changes in household composition and, in particular, family size. In 1851 a married couple headed most households and families were large. Both features were less pronounced in 1881. To be specific, in 1851 there were five times as many households in which the head was a married man living with his wife as there were households with a 'lone' head. ('Lone' heads are, for example, widow(er)s – often with unmarried children or lodgers in the household; or a bachelor or spinster – often living with other siblings.) By 1881 this ratio had fallen to about two to one. As regards family size in 1851 couples where the wife was aged 30-44 averaged 5.2 children under 15 living at home – by 1881 the comparable figure was 3.3 such children. By 1901 this had fallen to 2.0 children. Such a sharp fall in family size cannot wholly be attributed to the national trend to lower fertility; it also reflects the changing social structure of the area as its population grew.

2.4 Changes in age structure

The changes in the size of households and in their composition were linked to changes in the population's age structure. In 1841 and 1851 the population was relatively young. To quantify this it is safer to start with 1851 as the ages collected in 1841 may be suspect. Also it is more meaningful to exclude the living-in servants and comment on their numbers and ages separately. Of the resulting population in 1851 no less than nearly half (49%) were children under 15. This was a consequence of most married couples having fairly large families and there being few old people. Nobody was over 75 and only 14% of the population (one in seven) were 45 or more.

Figure 4(a) shows how much things had changed by 1881. Then the proportion of the population in the two youngest age groups had fallen – conversely the proportion in each of the older age groups had risen. This older age structure would be partly attributable to the age structure of those who had moved into the area. After 1881, because population growth – and in-migration – rose sharply there were further age structure changes as is evident from Figure 4(b). Comparing 1901 with 1881 the proportion of both children and the over-45s fell, while the proportions in the intervening age groups rose. This must have been the result of an influx of adults.

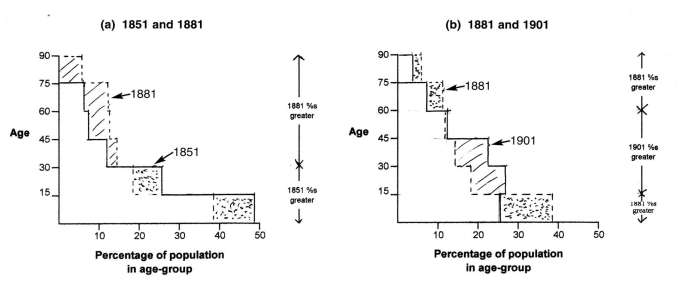

Figure 4. Age Structures, 1851, 1881 and 1901
(excluding servants)

2.5 Where people came from

None of the censuses included a question about residents' previous addresses – or where they had been in the preceding census. But there was a question about birthplace and this gives some clues about the population's geographical origins. Figure 5 shows some startling changes. First there is the change in the proportion of the population born in Surrey. In 1841 and 1851 this was around 90%. Thereafter, with the ever increasing population, the proportion fell steadily until in 1901 it was just over one-third. (The exception to the steady fall is 1871; but this fits on with the unusual population decline in the 1860s.) In terms of numbers, the population quadrupled between 1841 and 1901 while the number of Surrey born rose by just over one-half (60%) – much of which was in the first ten years. These patterns confirm that most of the population growth was due to people moving into the area from outside Surrey.

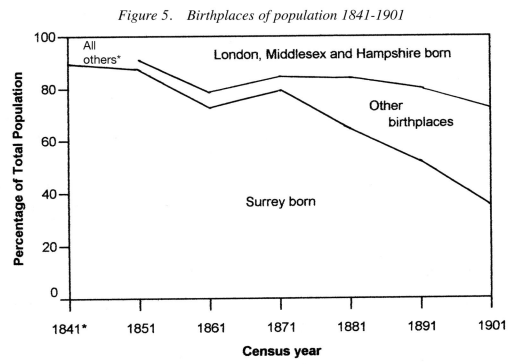

Figure 5. *Birthplaces of population 1841-1901*

* In 1841 no subdivision of those born outside Surrey was collected

Not only did the number, and proportion, of those born outside Surrey increase greatly between 1841 and 1901 but so did the extent of their catchment area. In 1851 twelve non-Surrey born people were enumerated. Nine of these had been born in the adjoining counties of Hampshire, London, and Middlesex (this analysis is not available for 1841) and the other three each came from a different English county. There was no one from the other countries of the United Kingdom or from abroad. In contrast by 1901 under half of the non-Surrey born inhabitants' birthplaces were Hampshire, London and Middlesex. The remainder were made up of 29 English counties together with Ireland, Scotland, Wales, Australia, Cape Colony, India and West Indies! (But there was no one born in the most distant English counties – Cornwall, Cumberland, Northumberland and Westmorland.)

Amongst the Surrey born too there is evidence of a greater propensity to travel. Persons born in Horsell parish accounted for three-quarters of the Surrey born in 1861 but by 1901 this proportion had been halved. (The 1851 breakdown has been ignored because the Horsell born were not always distinguished from the Surrey born. Thus many of those who were enumerated in both 1851 and 1861, *and* who were also recorded as Horsell born in 1861, had been recorded as Surrey born in 1851).

The birthplaces of young children can be a pointer to the timing of moves. For example one family were first enumerated in the area in 1861. They then had children aged 6 and 4 both of whom had been born in Peckham. So it is almost certain that the family had moved to Horsell within the preceding 4 years. Another family had a 2-year-old born in Horsell but four older siblings, the youngest of whom was 5, had been born in London. So this family had presumably moved between 2 and 5 years previously. Not all households have young children so this approach is of limited use.

2.6   Mobility

Evidently much of the population growth in the area was due to in-migration. A question that then arises is whether the incomers settled for a long stay or whether they soon moved on after a relatively short stay. The only census clues on this come from looking at the proportion of those present in one census who are again present in the next census. It is best to confine this calculation to heads of household aged under 65 at the first census – with the proviso that if a husband was head of household in the first census and his widow in the second this is not counted as a change. (This brings to mind the old *Punch* cartoon in which a small, weedy looking man is sitting at a table filling in his census form while beside him stands a large women saying in what is evidently a loud and threatening voice 'What do you mean – who is head of the household?') The age limit of 65 is imposed to reduce the influence of mortality; using only heads of household means the complications of children, or relations, leaving home is eliminated. What results is an indicator of changes/stability of ownership or tenancy of a property – but it is impractical to require this to be the same property as the census addresses were often too imprecise to ensure this.

The trend over time in this measure is revealing. Between both 1841-51 and 1851-61 the proportion of the heads of household to be found in the second census was over 60%; whereas for 1881-91 the figure was about 30% and for 1891-1901 was down to 20%. Note that this measure is not directly affected by the size of the inflow between the two censuses; it is an indicator of the extent of movement out of the area for those present at the first census. Deaths alone would mean the proportion could never be 100% but the sharp drop in the second half of the century is an indication of an increasingly mobile population. This is no surprise, as it is plausible that the likelihood of leaving an area is inversely related to the length of time a person has lived in the area; that is, newcomers are more likely to move out than longer-stayers. Hence as the proportion of newcomers rose the proportion of residents who moved out was also likely to rise. This trend would have been reinforced by the changes in social structure as the professional classes, for example, would be more likely to move out of the area than would labourers. A striking confirmation of this is that in only one of the gentlemen's residences was the same family to be found in successive censuses. It is also relevant that many properties were rented so moves were easier to arrange.

Arithmetically a family staying up to 20 years might be included in only one census – although they would usually be in two. But the 'one census' phenomenon is so common that the average stay must have been very much less than 20 years. Of course many who stayed less than 10 years would not be enumerated in any census.

3. Some Wider Social Aspects

3.1 Gentlemen's residences

The term gentlemen's residences is used as shorthand for large houses, standing in grounds of several acres, containing high status households with living-in servants. When the railway came, and indeed until after the 1851 census, there was only one such residence in the area – Kettlewell House on the top of the ridge at Kettlewell. This was a long established residence (see Appendix 4). By 1861 two new residences had appeared. One was again at Kettlewell while the other was almost as near the station as was possible while still being in Horsell. This was Alwyne House, just over the canal bridge, on whose site a Methodist church now stands – although the original grounds were much larger than the present church property. In each of the three 1861 residences both the husband and the wife had been born outside Surrey – five of the six in London or Middlesex. The husbands were probably Horsell's first commuters.

Table 2.   Gentlemen's residences – Population enumerated 1841-1901

	Number of persons						
Position in household	**1841**	**1851**	**1861**	**1871**	**1881**	**1891**	**1901**
Family and friends	2	0*	16	7	26	19	24
Servants and dependants							
Living-in	2	3	5	3	17	26	27
Living-out^	0	0	0	6	8	22	24
Total number of persons	**4**	**3**	**21**	**16**	**51**	**67**	**75**
Number of Residences inhabited	*1*	*1*	*3*	*2***	*5*	*6*	*8*

Notes:
*   In 1851 only servants and a visitor were enumerated.
**   In 1871 two residences were uninhabited.
^   Living-out servants and dependants. The head of household's occupation was that of coachman or gardener. Sometimes the address links the household head to a particular residence. When there is no such link the servant might have been employed by a household outside the Wheatsheaf area – or by a household not occupying a gentleman's residence. Both possibilities are unlikely. (Conversely there may have been servants who worked within the area but lived outside it. It is impossible to identify them.)

More new residences appeared in successive censuses. In 1871 it was Broom Hall (later spelt as one word) facing the recreation ground; this is still standing although subdivided and much altered. Then in 1881 Graylands was included while Kettlewell House was upgraded and renamed as Horsell Grange. Graylands (listed in 1881 as 'Greysend House') was built on part of a field (part of plot 91 in Figure 2) separated from Kettlewell Lane by a strip of the common; access across the common evidently was not then a problem! Graylands was the last gentleman's residence to be built on the lower, flatter, land between the foot of Kettlewell Hill and the canal. Whereas on Kettlewell Hill itself large houses were built up to the 1901 Census and subsequently (in 1891 came Lyndhurst and in 1901 Horsell Lodge and another which, confusingly, revived the old, discarded, name of Kettlewell House). So by 1901 there were eight gentlemen's residences in the Wheatsheaf area – five of which were on the ridge at Kettlewell. An idea of the character of these residences is given in Appendices 4 and 5 (which relate to Alwyne House and Graylands).

Table 2 quantifies the aggregate changes. After 1851 there was a steady growth in the number of residences and the number of residents; an exception was a drop in 1871 when two residences were empty. After 1881 the growth in total population was due to the increased number of servants and their dependants – the numbers of 'Family and friends' remained fairly steady.

As already mentioned a characteristic of the gentlemen's residences was a relatively rapid turnover of occupants. The only long stay family was the Comptons of Alwyne House. In no other residence was the same family enumerated in successive censuses.

3.2 Domestic living-in servants

As well as servants in the gentlemen's residences there were others living and working in more modest dwellings. Indeed for any 19th Century family with social pretensions at least one domestic servant was essential – even if only a 13-year-old skivvy from the workhouse. The number of servants employed was a rough guide to social status and, although the one or two servant households were the most numerous, those in the professional classes, and the more substantial businessmen, would usually aim to employ at least three servants. (Horn 1995: 22)

Key statistics about the living-in servants enumerated in the area, distinguishing between those in gentlemen's residences and others, are given in Table 3. Nearly all these servants were females though some living-out servants, such as coachmen or gardeners, were men. Until 1871 the number of servants in the area was in single figures and had not changed much since 1841; nor had the number of households with servants. The big increase in households had been in those without live-in servants.

Table 3. Living-in Servants 1841-1901

	1841	1851	1861	1871*	1881	1891	1901
Households – numbers							
Gentlemen's residences	1	1	3	2*	5	6	8
Others (with servants)	3	2	3	3	3	7	18
Without servants	9	15	18	23	21	25	49
Servants – numbers							
in gentlemen's residences	2	2	5	3	17	20	27
in others	3	3	3	3	3	12	25
Average number of servants							
Gentlemen's residences	2	2	1.7	1.5	3.4	3.3	3.4
Others (with servants)	1	1.5	1	1	1	1.7	1.4
Percentage of households with servants (excl gentlemen's residences)	*25*	*12*	*14*	*12*	*13*	*22*	*27*
Percentage of servants aged 25 or over	*40*	*20*	*25*	*33*	*35*	*44*	*42*
Percentage of servants born outside Surrey	*40*	*0*	*50*	*50*	*70*	*66*	*65*

* In 1871 two gentlemen's were uninhabited and so are not included.

By 1881 the picture had changed. There was a big increase in the number of servants in the gentlemen's residences and there tended to be more servants in each household (including any living in dwellings in the grounds of the big house). Before 1881 no household had 3 or more servants, but in 1881 and 1891 there were three such households (and then six in 1901). Alwyne House was unusual in never having more than two servants whereas Broom Hall started with one in 1871 but had four in 1901. The maximum number recorded was seven at Horsell Grange in 1881; where children aged 1, 2, 3 and 6 were a contributory factor. (The servants' occupations were cook, nurse, under nurse, parlourmaid, housemaid, kitchenmaid and coachman.)

In 1891 the greater part of the increase in servants' numbers was in the other, less prestigious, households. This was repeated in 1901 when a particular feature was a big increase in the number of households with just one servant – another reflection that much of the 1891-1901 doubling in numbers was in middle, or lower middle, class, households. Even so in 1901 there were still more households without a servant than there were with a servant (or servants) – although the gap had narrowed.

From 1881 onwards the proportion of the servants born outside Surrey was as high as, and fairly steady at, about two-thirds. It was part of the received Victorian wisdom for good household management that it was not wise to have local servants who, it was thought, would be likely to spread gossip about a household and also might be easily distracted from their duties by parents, suitors or friends. Also households moving into the area would often bring their servants with them. By 1901 there were servants born in Cape Colony, India, West Indies, Ireland as well as many from English counties.

The great majority of living-in servants were unmarried females so not surprisingly the majority, throughout the period, were under 25. But Table 3 shows that the proportion of those aged 25 or over was increasing and, from 1881 on, servants in their 30s or 40s were not unknown. At the other end of the scale there were a few 13 and 14-year-olds but their numbers were never large.

3.3   Farms

The 1851 records have three farms in the area – all at Kettlewell. The grandest, at the top of the hill, had both a name (Kettlewell Farm) and a gentleman's residence (Kettlewell House) associated with it. The other, nameless, farms were towards the bottom of the southern slope facing each other across Kettlewell Lane. The three farmhouses are probably the dwellings marked at Kettlewell on the old maps (see Section 1.2).

Ryde's 1851 records show Kettlewell Farm as having about 39 acres with Henry Roake as both owner and occupier. The 1851 Census also has an entry for Kettlewell Farm giving its occupant as an agricultural labourer; no details of acreage or the workforce were recorded. Possibly the farmer, presumably Henry Roake, lived at Kettlewell House. Although 1851 is the only Census that has an entry for 'Kettlewell Farm', farming as an economic activity evidently continued, for in 1871, and again in 1881, a farm bailiff was enumerated; there was no such person in the 1891 Census. This is in keeping with the evidence from the OS maps. The 1871 map marks the farm and the surrounding fields and these are listed as such in the Parish Area Book (see Appendix 2). But the 1896 OS map shows many of the fields as subdivided with some subdivisions having houses – see Figure 7(b). Finally, in Kelly's directories the farm is listed in the 1887 Directory but not in the 1890 Directory. So it looks as if the farm ceased to function in the late 1880s or early 1890s – shortly after Kettlewell House was modernised and extended to become Horsell Grange (see Appendix 4).

The farm at the foot of Kettlewell Hill, on the eastern side of Kettlewell Lane, was owned by the Fenn family. A widow, Olive Fenn, was the head of household with the occupation of 'farmer' in the 1841, 1851, and 1861 Censuses. The farm had been left to a son, John, prior to 1841 and his mother was his tenant. No details were given about the farm in 1841 but in 1851 it was 46 acres and employed 2 men and 1 boy. By 1861 the farm had a name (Vale Farm) although its size had fallen to 32 acres while the workforce was unchanged. By 1881 the name had grown to Kettle Vale Farm and John Fenn was the head of household with an occupation given as 'Independent'. In 1891 John Fenn was again enumerated in what must have been the same house but the word 'farm' had been dropped. However, unlike Kettlewell Farm, the 1896 map still shows the fields as undeveloped; although most are marked as 'Nurseries' whereas in 1871 they had been 'Arable' or 'Pasture'.

The farm opposite the Fenns' had the largest acreage of the three but the farmhouse was the first to disappear. In 1851 there was a tenant farming 60 acres and employing 3 labourers but neither in 1861 nor subsequently is there any mention of a farmer. Most of its fields featured on the 1871 OS map so must have been being farmed from elsewhere. The 1896 map shows a sizeable building on the site of the farmhouse – presumably a gentleman's residence.

3.4   Wheatsheaf Inn

That the Inn was not an ancient one is proven by its absence from the lists of licensed victuallers that are available (SHC 5/10/1) from 1785 to 1827. Then the legislation changed so there are no records to show when the Inn was first licensed but there is no trace of it in the 1841 Census. Nor was there a direct reference in the 1851 Census although there was a 'beer retailer' living in a dwelling described, as were several others, as 'NE of Chobham Road' – not today's Chobham Road. This was Reuben Percy who later ran the Albion Hotel in Woking and became a prominent local entrepreneur. It may be no coincidence that an engineer and a blacksmith were enumerated as visitors to his household.

Unlike the Census, the 1851 map (Figure 2) does mark the 'Wheat Sheaf Pub. Ho.' and its Book of Reference (Appendix 1) has the entry 'Wheat Sheaf Beer Ho and Gdn' with a John Percy as the occupier. This difference from the Census may be due to the business having opened during the year – or possibly Ryde was just more particular. In addition the Book of Reference shows an Arthur Smithers as the owner of the Beer House. His name is significant for he had been enumerated in the area in 1841 with the occupation of 'bricklayer'; he was enumerated in each Census until 1881 with occupations that included 'master bricklayer' and 'builder and grocer'. He seems to have been a speculative builder who built the public house and the two nearby cottages – Ryde recorded him as the owner of all these in 1851 when their Census location was given as Smither's (*sic*) Row. The physical size of the Beer House property was very small (about 1/8th of an acre) – much the same as the two cottages. The Land Tax records confirm both Arthur Smithers' involvement and that the buildings were new. For in 1851 his name is not mentioned but in 1852 there is an entry, that must be for the public house, with Arthur Smithers as owner and John Percy as occupier. The description of the property in the Land Tax records is 'House and premises'. The mention of 'premises' is unusual as is the omission of a reference to a garden; the amount of tax being paid was appreciably more than for an ordinary house. Later Land Tax records show that Arthur Smithers remained the owner of the Beer House, as well as of several houses and cottages, for some years.

By the time of the 1861 Census the business had expanded for a 'victualler' was listed as living at premises called 'Wheatsheaf'; eight other dwellings were listed as 'Near Wheatsheaf'. That by then 'the Wheatsheaf' was a recognised landmark is evident from an entry in the Manorial Court Roll for 1863 (SHC G97/4/5 p263) that refers to a premises in Broomhall Road as being 'near the Wheatsheaf' – but no earlier examples in the Manorial Rolls have been found. Indeed only a little earlier – in 1857 – Spencer Compton, the owner of Alwyne House, added an acre to his grounds and the geographical reference used in the Rolls was 'near to Horsell Wharf'.

In the 1871 Census the one word 'Wheatsheaf' was again used for the dwelling of a publican but the OS map of that date – see Figure 7(a) – reverts to the older spelling and marks 'Wheat Sheaf (PH)' with a cricket ground opposite. (Section 3.7 has more details about this piece of ground.) The wording in 1881 and 1891 was 'The Wheatsheaf'. The term 'Inn' was used in Kelly's 1890 Directory with the information that there was 'accommodation for beanfeasts & for boating, cricket, fishing and all outdoor sports'. That accommodation did not mean bedrooms but rooms for drink and food is clear from an official 1892 listing (SHC 5/10/22) of Surrey's 'fully-licensed houses and beer houses'. This included 'Wheatsheaf' as an Inn but has blanks in the columns for accommodation and stabling; the clientele were recorded as 'Labouring Classes'. The equivalent publication for 1904 (SHC 5/10/23) recorded that there was no sleeping accommodation – unusual for a fully licensed Inn – while there was stabling for 4 horses. The present, larger, building dates from the 1930s and was the work of Stephen Silk, a well known Horsell builder. As well as the old Inn one or two old cottages were demolished.

The name Wheatsheaf came from an older property nearer the canal. The 1834 Parish Survey lists a field named Wheatsheaf Mead and a Wheatsheaf House. Then the index to the 1851 map gives Wheatsheaf Mead as the name of the field numbered 120 on Figure 2. The occupiers of plots 118 and 119 are also to be found in the 1851 Census with the address 'Wheatsheaf Cottages'. Thus there can be no doubt that this is the origin of the name Wheatsheaf and that it had been in use since before 1834. Indeed the dwellings are very likely those shown in this vicinity on the 1816 OS map. The use of 'Wheatsheaf Cottages' rather than 'Wheatsheaf House' in 1851 is not a problem for house names in the 19th Century had not been formalised except for the larger residences. Also the 1851 index describes the properties as 'Tenements and Gardens'; one of the dictionary definitions of a tenement is 'a portion of a house, tenanted as a separate dwelling' so Wheatsheaf Cottages in one census could easily be Wheatsheaf House in another – or vice-versa.

3.5 Schoolteachers

One of the few non-agricultural household heads in 1841 was a schoolteacher – James Furner. He was enumerated with his wife, a baby and a family servant. The couple were in their 20s. They were again enumerated in 1851 when the household had grown to include 6 children and a cousin (in addition to the couple and a servant). Children who were aged 4 or more were listed as 'Scholar at home'. The husband, wife, and cousin were each entered as 'British teachers' – a term which may need some explanation. In the early 19th Century a philanthropist, Joseph Lancaster, had been so concerned about the lack of education for children of the poor that he set out to do something about it. His ideas caught on and resulted in an organisation called The British and Foreign Schools Society (BFSS). This flourished in the first half of the 19th century but then became redundant with the spread of state schools – in Horsell the national school opened in 1851. The archivist of the BFSS replied to a request for information about the Furners as follows:

> If the three Furners were listed as 'British teachers' in the census returns, this almost certainly means that they were teachers at a British School(s). It was quite common for a husband and wife to be Master and Mistress of a school with he being responsible for the boys and she for the girls and infants. It would not be unusual for a further member of the family (in this case Charlotte) to be an assistant teacher. There is no indication that any was trained at Borough Road, the British and Foreign School Society College, so they were probably in 1851 'uncertificated' teachers, i.e. they had not been to college and therefore not gained the teachers' certificate. Indeed in 1851 the vast majority of teachers were 'uncertificated'.

> We have now found that there was a British School at Horsell. The only information we have on it, however (from a list of closed British schools published by the BFSS in 1897), was that the Horsell school was founded around 1829. (*Personal communication*)

As the school was founded in 1829 the Furners, who were only in their twenties in 1841, could not have been its first teachers. Nothing is known about the earlier teachers. However the 1851 map (Figure 2) shows a school on the site on which, in the late 1850s, Alwyne House was built; it seems likely that this was the Furners' school. The 1851 property included a Baptist chapel as well as an inhabited dwelling; the plot was just over 2 acres so there were some grounds as well as the buildings.

No teacher was enumerated in the area in 1861 but in 1871 there was a Miss Anne Nealds – a 57-year-old spinster schoolmistress who was living alone. The first trace of her in the Land Tax records is for 1865 when she had moved into one of Arthur Smithers's cottages – very likely one of those near the Wheatsheaf Inn as her 1871 Census entry immediately follows that for the Inn. Ten years later she had been joined by three younger sisters and a niece, all unmarried and all with an occupation entered as 'Governess Private Schoolmistress'; again the listing was next to the Inn's and on the canal side. Given that she was listed as living in a 'Cottage and garden' the school could not have been a large one. The street directories record Miss Nealds or Neel (the spelling varies) as running a 'ladies' school'; she is included in the directories for 1867, 1874, and 1882 but not in that 1887. Thus the school seems to have been open from the mid-1860s until the 1880s.

There was no school in the 1891 Census but in 1901 there was again a school. This was in a house, built in the early 1890s, on the corner of Chobham Road and Ferndale Road. The Census lists three unmarried sisters, and an unrelated spinster, as 'schoolteachers'. The mother of the sisters, a widow, was the head of the household; which also included a 15-year-old 'school boarder' and two servants.

With its increasing population it is not surprising that there was a private school by the 1871s; it is more curious that there was one in the 1830s and 1840s.

3.6 Basingstoke Canal

Only a short stretch of the canal lies within the Wheatsheaf area. Even so it is remarkable that in just one of the seven censuses was anyone living or working on the canal enumerated. This exception is the inclusion, in 1871, of the occupants of a canal barge. The owner, William Strudwick, was 'absent' but his wife Mary Ann and their 4 children together with William's (or maybe Mary Ann's) sister and her 3 children were present. Probably the barge was moored at or near Horsell Wharf. This was one of the ten public wharves along the canal at which goods could be loaded or unloaded. A storehouse is marked on Ryde's 1851 map – numbered 111 in Figure 2. The wharf's main claim to fame is that the first ever cargo carried on the canal, a 28 ton load, was delivered to Horsell in 1791.

The wharf was some 200 yards west of the canal bridge – no trace of it remains. The site was not the most convenient place for Horsell village but was convenient for its proximity to the Guilford–Chertsey road. It is strange that the wharf was not nearer the road – maybe there was some feature such as drainage that determined this. The wharf was used by census enumerators from 1871 on to describe the location of some nearby labourers' cottages. This area is marked, but not named, on the OS maps (Section 4.2 has more details). The canal itself was used as a geographical feature to describe the location of dwellings in some censuses – not least because, as already mentioned, historically a small part of the parish was on the southern (town and railway) side of the canal.

Figure 6.   Wheatsheaf Bridge in the early 1900s

The bridge is viewed from the station side. A brick parapet can be seen to the left of the motor car. The houses on the right were built in the 1890s – see Section 4.6. See also Figure 10 for a photograph taken on the other side of the bridge.

The 1851 Book of Reference describes the canal bridge as Horsell Bridge. This, or Horsell Wharf Bridge, was also the name used by the canal people of the late 19th Century – which would have been the most obvious name when the bridge was built, around 1796, given its close proximity of the wharf which served Horsell. (*Personal communication from Tony Harmsworth* re his grandfather and great grandfather who both worked on the canal. The latter would have started work in the 1850s.) The OS however opted for 'Wheatsheaf Bridge' for their maps from 1871 onwards. Interestingly H G Wells in 'War of the Worlds' mentions Horsell Bridge several times. Admittedly this could have been to simplify his geographical references; but it may have been how the locals referred to the bridge at that time.

The original 1792 brick, narrow, hump-backed bridge was not well maintained by the impoverished canal company and anyway by the early 1900s was inadequate for the growing volume of traffic and the advent of the motor car. The kind of traffic jam that resulted is shown in Figure 6. Consequently the bridge had to be rebuilt – this should have been the canal company's responsibility but Woking UDC eventually had to pay.

3.7   Horsell (or Wheatsheaf) Recreation Ground

This recreation ground does not feature in the censuses but it affects the character of the area so it is sensible to outline its origins. The first relevant record is on the 1871 OS map – Figure 7(a) – which has an almost square piece of land on Horsell Moor opposite Broom Hall marked as 'Cricket Ground'. If drawn to scale this was about 44 yards across so would not be large enough to include the outfield but is more likely to be the area on which the wickets could be pitched. By the time of the 1896 OS map the cricket ground had disappeared and its location had become just part of the Moor.

However there are SHC records (G97/4/22) of correspondence in 1892/93 about an agreement between Lord Onslow and some local worthies. What was under consideration was that part of the present recreation ground extending from Chobham Road to the far end of Ferndale Road – about 10 acres. To quote '… permission is asked, to be allowed to level and lay down turf such portion of the ten acres as may be deemed requisite for cricket or football.'

Presumably the surface that had been played on around 1871 was too rough. Care had to be taken not to offend the aristocratic landowner Lord Onslow ' … no desire or intention to encroach further upon the rights of the Lord of the Manor, or the commoners'.

Evidently quite a lot of work was required as '… it will be necessary to expend a substantial sum in levelling and laying down in turf.'

Funds were to be raised by public subscription. Elsewhere it is commented that 'the parish is not a wealthy one' which may be why only half of the 10 acres were converted into a recreation ground. There are several mentions in the correspondence of 'the games of Cricket and football' (capital letter for one game but not the other!); also some of the letters are headed 'Horsell Cricket Ground' – so maybe cricket was the major game or at any rate the one most favoured by the letter writers. There is reference to the need to 'protect the cricket pitch in some way' which led later to a request that as well as 'moveable posts or chains' that 'hurdles' should be allowed. The ground is consistently referred to as the Horsell – and not as the Wheatsheaf – recreation ground. The first trustees were two gentlemen from large residences on Kettlewell which hints at the lack any suitable long established gentry living nearer Horsell village to take such an initiative. That the 1896 map does not mark the area may be because it took a year or two to raise the funds and have the work done.

A few years later (in 1908) there was a bout of correspondence trying to decide who should pay for the making-up of the adjoining Ferndale Road. No figures are given but presumably the cost was being divided between the owners of the two sides of the road. The trustees granted the lease by Lord Onslow did not think it fell within their responsibility; Lord Onslow did not think he should pay as the land was of no value to him; and Woking UDC did not want to buy the land but their clerk thought the Council might waive the charge in exchange for Lord Onslow giving up his rights over the 10 acres. The matter was resolved fairly quickly for Woking UDC soon agreed to the making-up.

After the Second World War the recreation ground was extended to include a second football pitch.

Figure 7(a).   OS Map of the Wheatsheaf area in 1871

(Reproduced from the 1871 Ordnance Survey map; the scale of this copy is 1 inch represents about 120 yards. See Appendix 2 for a key to the plot numbers.)

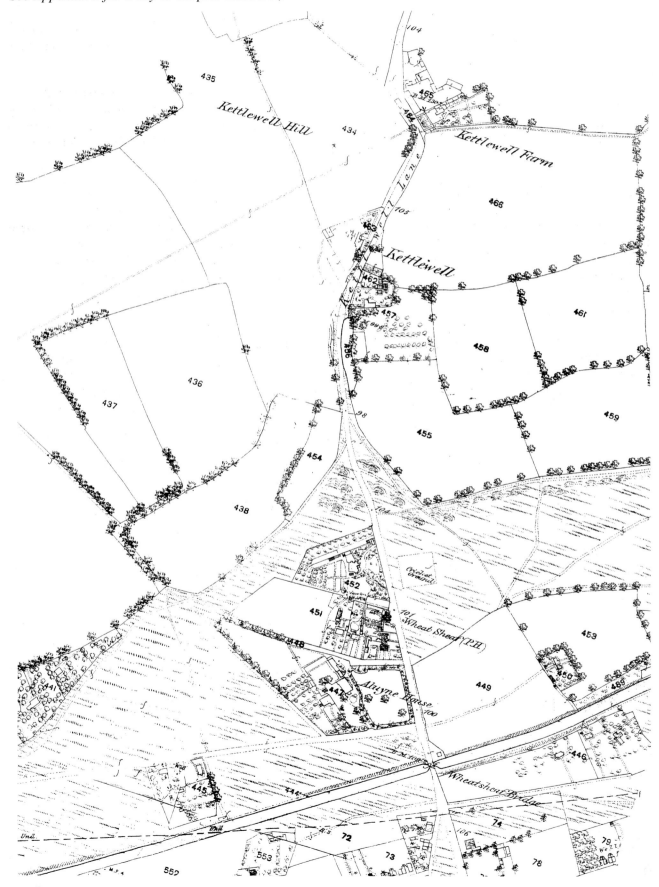

Figure 7(b).   OS Map of the Wheatsheaf area in 1896

(Reproduced from the 1896 Ordnance Survey map; the scale of this copy is 1 inch represents about 120 yards.)

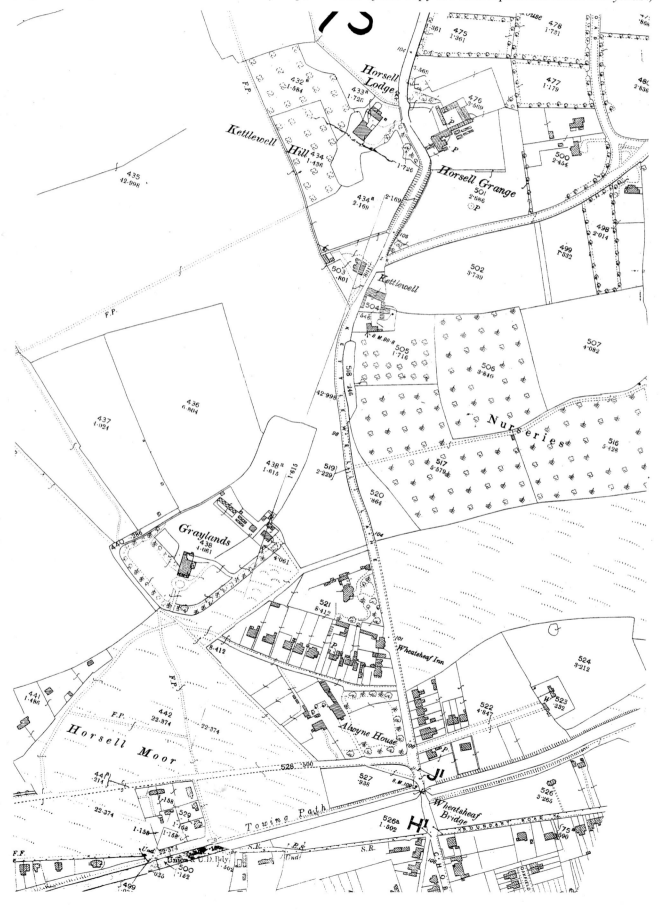

3.8 Common land

The 1851 map (Figure 2) shows that the land between the fields on the slopes of Kettlewell Hill and the canal was predominantly common land with dwellings occupying only a small proportion of the area. However, as time passed, encroachments were made. For example the 1871 OS map shows that common land had been lost to an enlargement of the Alwyne House plot, to the building of Broom Hall and some dwellings along Broomhall Road, and to the creation of an arable field between Wheatsheaf House and Chobham Road. By 1896 some common land between Graylands and the road had been enclosed; as had some near Alwyne House.

The vegetation of the common land would, unlike today's, have been an almost treeless heath – and was so marked on the OS maps. At the turn of the century a sales brochure stressed '... the splendid range of Heather-covered commons stretching for thousands of acres ...'. That this was a striking feature to the new residents is evident from the names given to two of the older houses on Broomhall Road. The one nearest to the heath was called Heathview while the owner of, or maybe the builder selling, the next but one exercised a little creative imagination in choosing the name Heathside. Even a 1930's house was called Heather Court.

The transition from common land in a rural backwater to common land in suburbia would not be without its problems. This is evident from a report in the *Surrey Advertiser* of 22nd October 1881 concerning a fight on Horsell Common between gamekeeper and a local man over shooting rights. The local (Edward Roake) claimed he had a legal right to shoot and had done so for 20 years. The gamekeeper disagreed; he was employed by Richard Brettell the occupant, in the 1881 Census, of Horsell Grange (formerly Kettlewell House) who was a well known local solicitor.

4.   Changes up to 1901 by locality

4.1   Limitations of the information available

The censuses often give insufficient information to identify exactly where people lived. For example in 1841 of the 13 dwellings listed, two are described as Kettlewell and the other 11 quite correctly, if rather unhelpfully, as Horsell. Subsequent censuses give progressively more detail but even in 1891 only the house names of the larger dwellings were recorded (and these cannot always now be identified). Moreover in each census the dwellings could be listed in a slightly different order as the route an enumerator took to cover his area was at his discretion.

The 1851 map (Figure 2) and its Book of Reference (Appendix 1) add a detailed geographical dimension to the 1851 Census – which means well-founded deductions can be made about other censuses. (A preliminary is to go back from 1851 to 1841 when there were 4 fewer dwellings. As explained in Section 3.4 it is reasonable to conclude that three of these were the Public House and its two associated cottages; the fourth cannot be identified.) From 1871 onwards the series of large scale OS maps – Figures 7(a) and (b) – often help by showing features recorded by the enumerator. The Sections that follow describe the changes in different parts of the area. As usual the censuses provide the detail about the social changes. Developments after 1901 are, in the main, left until Section 5.

4.2   Horsell Moor and The Wharf

The first census to mention The Moor was that of 1861. The dwellings concerned were the buildings shown on Ryde's 1851 map on plots 107, 108 and 109 (not shown on Figure 2). The 1871 and 1896 OS maps combine the three 1851 plots into one (plot 441); the 1896, and later, OS maps label the common land adjoining the cottages, which is on the northern side of Brewery Road, as 'Horsell Moor'. Access was from an old track across the common.

There were four dwellings in 1851 as one of the three buildings was a tenement of two dwellings. The 1841 Census does not give enough geographical information to identify the dwellings but three of the four known 1851 households were enumerated so it seems likely that at least three of the four dwellings existed in 1841. The 1851 dwellings can be found in the 1871, 1881, and 1891 censuses (and were doubtless included in 1861 but the geographical information is insufficient). After 1891 these dwellings began to disappear. There was one dwelling less in the 1901 Census and by the time of the 1912 OS map another had gone. Plot 441 eventually became part of the back gardens of houses in Horsell Park.

Ryde's 1851 records show the dwellings were not owned by their occupiers; while the Census shows that the heads of household were mostly labourers – and there was some continuity in the occupants. An extreme example is that a Henry Howard or his son was enumerated in every census from 1841 to 1901. The older man died in a workhouse and both men were always entered as labourers – initially as agricultural labourers but later as nursery garden labourers (the same change as on the OS maps for many of the nearby fields). Ryde recorded the size of the plots as 0.88 acre (shared between the two semi-detached dwellings), 0.4 acre and 0.18 acre. So even the smallest had a good sized garden by today's standards – the others were definitely large.

Another group of cottages was at The Wharf – first mentioned in the 1871 Census. The term came to refer to the dwellings marked on the 1871 map – Figure 7(a) – on plot 445. This area is also marked on Ryde's 1851 map (plot 110) when there was just one dwelling which was inhabited by an owner-occupier (Isaac Hampton). Isaac had been enumerated in 1841 though it is uncertain if it was in the same dwelling as his place in the sequence of householders is unusual. The plot's size in 1851 was 0.86 acres. By 1871 this area had grown to 1.16 acres. The 1881 and 1891 Censuses both record six dwellings with the address of 'The Wharf'. The timing of the 1851-1881 increase is uncertain but looking at the census records there could have been perhaps 3 dwellings in 1861 and 6 in 1871 (the addresses are too vague to be definite). In the 1901 Census the number dropped to 4. This is odd because the 1896 OS map shows 6 buildings and the 1912 map shows 7. The 1934 map also shows 7 but the footprints of most of the buildings were very different. There had been extensive redevelopment with many of the new buildings among those that are there today. However the original 1851 building is still marked on the same site in 1934 and may be the cottage shown in Figure 8. Thus the Wharf's underlying trend has been one of development and redevelopment – unlike the cottages on The Moor which simply disappeared.

Figure 8. A Labourer's cottage

This thatched cottage, known as 'Overholme', stood in the Wharf area; believed to have been photographed in the early 1960s. The man is a Mr Hampton. The Hampton family appear in every Census, probably living in this cottage, from 1851 to 1901. In the Street Directory for 1949-50 there are 9 dwellings listed at The Wharf – 3 of which were occupied by a Hampton.

As with the Moor the 19th Century heads of household were mostly labourers and there was some inter-censal continuity. On both The Wharf and The Moor the dwellings themselves would almost certainly have been traditional cottages. Figure 8 shows a cobb cottage that stood until the 1960s and remained in the possession of the Hampton family until then. (*Personal communication from Mrs Parfitt.*)

In 1891 and 1901 census enumerators were instructed to record 'the number of rooms if less than five'. Of the ten dwellings in the two areas in 1891 four were in this category; and in 1901 five out of seven were. Proportionately more of the small cottages were on the Wharf; and intriguingly the original Isaac Hampton's son was in the smallest with just 2 rooms in 1901. It is not at all surprising that many labourers' cottages were small; what is surprising is that their sizes varied so much. In 1901 there were cottages listed with 2, 3, and 4 rooms – as well as the remainder with 5 or more rooms.

4.3 Brewery Road – Carpark and Kingswood Court

These plots form a strip of land that lies between the canal and Brewery Road – bounded at one end by the Wharf and at the other by Chobham Road. The 1851 and 1871 maps show the whole of the area as common land. By 1896 the Kingswood Court site-to-be (plot 527) had been acquired by the owners of Alwyne House.

In the late 1920s, when the Alwyne House estate was up for auction, the plot was one of the lots but was not built on until the 1960s. The future carpark plot remained as common land until 1930 when Woking UDC bought the land, described as being common or waste lands of the manor of Pyrford, from the Earl of Onslow. Subsequently the land was used for allotments – as can be seen from the frontispiece – and then became a carpark. Plans for use of the site for a hotel, a church, and a new County Hall for Surrey have come and gone.

4.4   South of the canal

In 1841 Horsell Parish included some land south of the canal bridge. Here, to the east of Chobham Road and some distance from it, the 1851 map shows two dwellings (on plots 115 and 117). Both plots were just over one acre and both had owner-occupiers who were agricultural labourers. Ten years later the occupants were unchanged and, although the dwellings cannot be identified in every census, the signs are that there was some permanency of occupation. In the 1891 and 1901 Censuses the two dwellings had graduated to having names – unlike the cottages on The Moor and The Wharf. By 1901 the Cottage Hospital had been built on land between these cottages and the canal bridge – and this piece of land had ceased to be in Horsell Parish. Not surprisingly by the time of the 1912 OS map the dwellings had disappeared with the development of housing along Boundary Road. The small triangle of land on the west of Chobham Road remained, for a time, in Horsell parish but was never inhabited.

4.5   Chobham Road – West Side

Until the 1890s all the developments on Chobham Road before Kettlewell were on the western side. Ryde's 1851 map shows the Wheat Sheaf Public House and three cottages on plots 114 and 113 – each newly built (details in Section 3.4). Then on plot 112 there was a Chapel and School in 1851; so this plot may have been the site of the buildings shown in this vicinity on the 1816 OS map. The 1851 Religious Census lists a Baptist Chapel in Horsell 'opposite the Woking railway station'. There being no other alternative this must be the Chapel on plot 112 even though the station is some 400 yards away; presumably there was a lack of alternative prominent objects! The chapel is recorded as having been erected in 1848 with sittings for 164 people and 150 children in the gallery. Average attendance in 1851 was 180 in the morning (including children) and 100 in the evening. These are very large numbers for a sparsely populated area. It is also a mystery how it came about that that barely ten years after it had been erected the Chapel (and School) made way for Alwyne House.

The 1871 OS map shows how the 1851 plots had been much extended and linked up by incorporating common land. Also, along the northern boundary of the grounds of Alwyne House there was a new road (Broomhall Road); this left Chobham Road by following the 1851 boundary but then deviated in a way which increased the extent of Alwyne House's grounds. On the northern side of this road several cottages had been erected. Then on Chobham Road, but nearer Kettlewell, Broom Hall had been built on land carved out of the common.

The only substantial change in the 1870s was the construction of Graylands but more extensive development took place in the 1880s. Most of the new dwellings were along Broomhall Road on the same triangle of land as Broom Hall and the inn. Previously in Broomhall Road there had only been workmen's houses. More were added in the 1880s but there were also, tactfully separated from the smaller houses by a builder's yard, five middle class detached houses on larger plots – four of which remain today. These houses were nothing like as large as the gentlemen's residences although each had one or two live-in domestic servants in 1891. This marks the start of an influx of what might be termed the middle middle class – in contrast to the upper middle class inhabitants of the gentlemen's residences. Thus by the 1890s the area around the Wheatsheaf Inn, with its reportedly labouring class clientele, was quite a mixture. Dotted amongst the dwellings of the better off were those of manual workers.

A puzzle concerning the geographical pattern of these developments is how the land for Alwyne House and Broom Hall, as well as the land in between them to which Broomhall Road gave access, became available for development. The area as a whole is an oddly shaped island – see Figure 7(b) – surrounded by the Waste to which it originally belonged (see Figure 2). That it was an enclosure is confirmed by the reference in early documents to Broomhall Road as an 'occupation road' – and in the Parish Area Book of 1871 as a 'Private road'.

Figure 9(a)   Plan of Wheatsheaf Estate, 1900

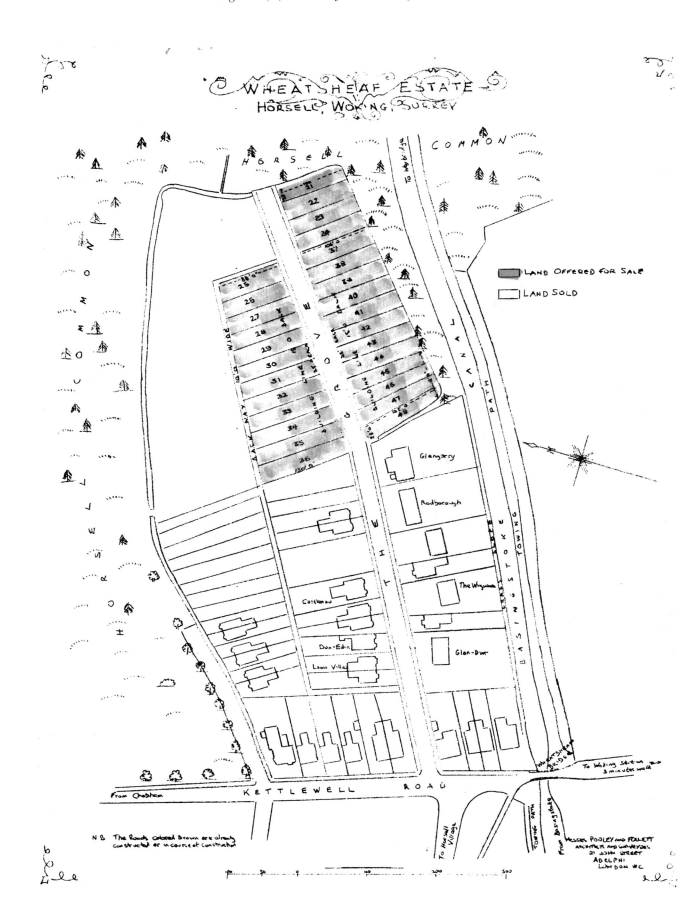

Figure 9(b)   Advertisement for the sale of Wheatsheaf Estate building land

WOKING, SURREY.

WHEATSHEAF ESTATE

OF

THE NATIONAL LAND CORPORATION, LIMITED.

Particulars, Plan and Conditions of Sale

OF

28 PLOTS OF RIPE

Freehold Building Land,

WHICH IS THE

ONLY AVAILABLE LAND NEAR WOKING SURROUNDED BY HORSELL COMMON.

About three minutes' walk from WOKING JUNCTION STATION, London and South-Western Railway.

ADMIRABLY ADAPTED FOR

WELL-DESIGNED VILLA RESIDENCES,

WITH GOOD GARDENS,

For which there is a great demand in this very favourite position.

Nine-tenths of the Purchase Money can be paid by instalments (if desired) extending over Ten Years.

FREE CONVEYANCES (STAMP DUTY EXCEPTED).

(See Conditions of Sale.)

MESSRS. F. G. WHEATLEY & SON

INSTRUCTED BY THE VENDORS,

The National Land Corporation, Limited,

Will offer the above by Auction at the RAILWAY HOTEL, WOKING,

On TUESDAY, the 27th of NOVEMBER, 1900,

At SIX o'clock p.m. precisely.

A limited number of RETURN RAILWAY TICKETS will be issued by the Auctioneers or Vendors, at the Reduced Fare of 2s. 6d. each.

Particulars, Plan and Conditions of Sale, can be obtained at the principal Hotels; of A. W. PEARCE, Esq., Solicitor, 21, John Street, Adelphi, W.C.; of the Vendors, **THE NATIONAL LAND CORPORATION, LIMITED,** 18, Adam Street, Adelphi; of the Estates Agency, Limited, Woking Station; and of the Auctioneers, at

28 & 29, CHANCERY LANE. W.C.

4.6 Chobham Road – East side

The 1851 map shows all the land on the eastern side of Chobham Road, until the fields on the slope of Kettlewell Hill, as common land. There were however two isolated cottages (plots 118 and 119) in a field (plot 120) some distance from the road. As explained in Section 3.4 it was from these dwellings, and the field, that the name Wheatsheaf originated. Their household heads in 1851 were an agricultural labourer and an elderly widow (listed as a pauper) so there is no obvious reason why the dwellings, of which the occupants were tenants, were deserving of a name. Nor was the physical size of the plots unusual – 0.4 and 0.2 acres. The owner of the two plots also owned several nearby fields so the cottages were probably 'tied'. A minor puzzle is why the long established 'Wheatsheaf' name ceased to appear in the 1871 and subsequent censuses – particularly as the 1871 and 1896 OS maps show the cottages still existed.

The 1871 map also shows that the land between the field (plot 120) and the road was no longer common land but had been enclosed with the new field recorded as 5 acres of arable land. Presumably this new field was created for bona-fide agriculture or horticultural reasons as it was over 20 years before it was built on. There were no houses on this land in the 1891 Census. But by 1896 the OS map – Figure 7(b) – had four detached, and a pair of semi-detached, houses facing onto Chobham Road between The Grove and the point where Ferndale Road would be constructed a little later. In The Grove there were only three properties and that road is half its final length – with the Wheatsheaf House cottages still standing and inhabited.

That the Grove was developed as a whole is clear from Figure 9(a) and (b) – which relate to the position in 1900 and are copied from the sales brochure (SHC G113/4). The development was called Wheatsheaf Estate so the original name had not been entirely forgotten. The speed of development after 1896 is apparent from a comparison of Figure 9(a) with Figure 7(b). By 1900 most of the plots in the first half of the Grove had been built on – and three pairs of 'semis' had been erected along what would become Ferndale Road. Plot sizes varied. Some, but not all, of those on the canal (south) side of the Grove were similar to the earlier Broomhall Road five; those on the north side of the Grove were smaller while the Ferndale Road semis had yet narrower plots. The plots being auctioned in 1900 were fairly narrow although the purchaser of a plot had the right to buy the adjoining one at the same price.

The 1901 Census reveals something about those moving into the recently built houses. Their social standing roughly corresponded to the sizes of the plots. Thus in Ferndale Road (in the 1901 Census this name was not used – the dwellings were listed as numbers 1 to 6 Park View) three of the six semis contained two households and another two had households that included boarders. So only one of the six had a basic family household (it contained an 85-year-old widow and two spinster daughters). The heads of household with jobs were mostly skilled craftsmen and superior tradespeople – e.g. a milliner, coppersmith, journeyman baker. None of these Ferndale Road households included a servant. Whereas in The Grove the houses on the canal side of were occupied by 'professional' heads of household (e.g. a Captain in the 13th Hussars and an architect) and several had servants. Those on the other side of the road were more mixed – one had two households and another two included boarders while some of the others had servants. The houses on Chobham Road had a mixture of 'professional' heads (e.g. a veterinary surgeon and an analytical chemist) and superior tradesmen (e.g. a draper shopkeeper listed as an employer with an assistant living in and a plumber/decorator). The house on the corner of Chobham Road and Ferndale Road was a school (see Section 3.5).

Figure 9(b) shows the sales techniques in use at the turn of the century. A developer was at work and marketed his product professionally – with several selling points including the offer of low-cost train tickets and an after-work time for the auction. Commuters were seen as a target market – the sales brochure gave the times of all the Woking to Waterloo (and vice-versa) train times as well as the information, in bold block capitals, that there was 'direct communication with the city by the new city and Waterloo electric railway'. Another selling point was 'the health-giving air from the Pine Woods' – not to mention the appeal to the pocket in that the rating of Horsell Parish 'is very considerably below that of Woking'. A sign of the times was that electricity and gas were optional extras. There are also points of interest on the map. No recreation ground was marked – in agreement with the 1896 OS map – instead the land was marked as 'Horsell Common'; Ferndale Road had been started but not named; today's Chobham Road was called Kettlewell Road (not Lane); the term Wheatsheaf Estate was used – perhaps to give a favourable rural image.

Figure 10.   Chobham Road about 1900

The view was taken from just over the Wheatsheaf Bridge looking along Chobham Road towards Kettlewell. The card is postmarked 1909 and judging from the maturity of the hedges in front of the houses on the right, which were built in the early 1890s, the picture must have been taken in the 1900s. The entrance to The Grove is at the lamppost in the right foreground. Further away there is no sign of a break in the kerb for the entrance to Ferndale Road. The trees on the left were in the grounds of Alwyne House. The fingerpost reads 'Knaphill' and 'Bisley'.

To the north of the Wheatsheaf Estate was the common land that in the 1890s became a recreation ground – see Section 3.7. Further north, on the slopes of Kettlewell Hill, were the farms and farmland whose development was traced in Section 3.3.

4.7   Kettlewell

The pattern of development at Kettlewell is unclear because links between censuses, even for the residences, are hampered by inconsistencies in the house names. In 1861 there were two residences – Kettlewell House and Alicia (the spelling is problematic as the Census entry is barely legible) House. The latter may well have been built on the site of the farmhouse on the lower slopes of Kettlewell Hill which was recorded in the 1851 Census but then disappeared; the 1871 OS map has a building on the site of the farmhouse. Unfortunately in the 1871 Census it looks as if both residences were unoccupied as neither was listed but two uninhabited, and consequently unnamed, dwellings were noted.

In 1881 there were again two dwellings although their names differ from 1861's. One was The Grange (sometimes Horsell Grange) which replaced Kettlewell House – see Appendix 4 for the reasons for thinking this to be so. Alicia House seems to have been renamed Kettle Vale House – which became Kettlewell Vale in 1891.To the two 1881 residences were added one (Lyndhurst) in 1891 and two (Horsell Lodge and another) in 1901. Identifying the inter-censal links becomes more difficult as the number of houses increases because the house names used sometimes vary. Nor do the surnames of the occupants help as they, too, often differ in each census; a reminder of the fairly rapid turnover amongst the better-off residents.

At about the time Horsell Grange replaced Kettlewell House the surrounding fields were subdivided into the building plots shown on the 1896 map. A key player in this seems to have been a Richard Brettell who was living at Horsell Grange in the 1881 Census. He was a solicitor in a well known Chertsey partnership. He was involved in selling some of the fields that had been part of the farm associated with Horsell Grange to the National Land Company (SHC 7385/1). The same set of documents includes the sale in 1894 of four plots of land that are described as '... part of the Company's Horsell Grange Estate ...'. It was the National Land Company that auctioned the plots of land accessed from the Grove mentioned in the preceding Section – see Figure 9(b). Moreover the sales brochure for the Grove contained an advertisement for the auction of six plots of land, suitable for 'Residences of a Superior Class', on the Horsell Grange Estate. Many of the resulting dwellings were accessed from new tributary roads – Woodham Road going through the fields to the east had been constructed by 1896. For the reasons given earlier it was not judged necessary to include dwellings accessed from Woodham Road in this study.

5.   Developments after 1901

5.1   Overview

After 1901 resort must be made to sources such as the Ordnance Survey maps for 1912 and 1934, Street Directories, Kelly's Directories, electoral registers, planning documents and so on. These provide an idea of the way development continued but lack the censuses' social analyses. A simple count of the number of dwellings in the area is shown in Table 4. The comparability over time of the numbers is not exact because of the different sources that have been used – but the changes are so large that the general trend is reliable.

Table 4.   Numbers of Dwellings[1] 1901-2005

	1901[2]	1921[3]	1936[3]	1950[3]	1964[3]	1985[4]	2005[5]
Number of dwellings	75	142	306	380	602	927	1039
Percentage increase (since previous count)	*n/a*	*89*	*115*	*24*	*58*	*54*	*12*

Note:

1 Defined to be as comparable as possible with censuses. Hence only private residences were counted; flats were counted as separate dwellings even if they were subdivisions of an old house that had been a single dwelling.

Sources:

2 Census of Population.
3 Street Directories.
4 Electoral Register.
5 Visual inspection.

Take first the total number of dwellings. The unbroken upward trend is no surprise but the variations in the rate of increase are interesting. The most basic finding is that after the late 19th Century building boom the tendency has been for a declining growth rate. The increase for 1881-1901 was 159% so the increases for 1901-1921 and 1921-1936 (even allowing for the latter being only 15 years) were both a decrease. The 1936-1950 change was affected by the war and post-war austerity so is, historically, very low. But the 1950-1964 and the 1964-1985 increases are both less than earlier in the century while the 1985-2005 increase is not only another reduction but is even less than the 1936-1950 figure.

Broad spatial changes within the area are evident from the growth of the road network. The 1851 map (Figure 2) has just two roads – or more precisely tracks. All the dwellings were approached via one or the other of these tracks. When greenfield development began side, ie tributary, roads were soon needed to give access to more land. The 1871 OS map, Figure 7(a), shows the first such road was Broomhall Road – a modest start. Soon however larger scale development was in progress. By 1896 Woodham Road had been constructed to open up the eastern part of Horsell Grange Estate; and a start had been made on The Grove. By 1900 The Grove was partially developed and Ferndale had been started – see Section 4.6. By the time of the 1912 OS map Ferndale Road and The Grove are shown as almost, but not quite, as they are today.

Further away from the canal the 1912 OS map, Figure 11(a), shows several roads had been built to develop the western slopes of the Kettlewell ridge. Here the main tributary road was Horsell Rise. This, in turn, had secondary tributaries of Ridgeway and Church Road; and the latter had its own tributary of Fletcher Road. (In the 1930s this was changed to Horsell Vale – illustrating that the desire for a nice street name is not a new phenomenon. Fletcher was actually quite respectable being the name of a local 19th Century landowner.) The road network in 1924, with road names, is shown in Figure 1.

Access to the Kettlewell slopes from Brewery Road was via Horsell Park which was constructed immediately to the west of the Horsell Moor cottages. In 1912 there were still many empty plots along these tributary roads

Figure 11(a)   OS Map of the Wheatsheaf area in 1912

(Reproduced from the 1912 Ordnance Survey map; the scale of this copy is 1 inch represents about 120 yards.)

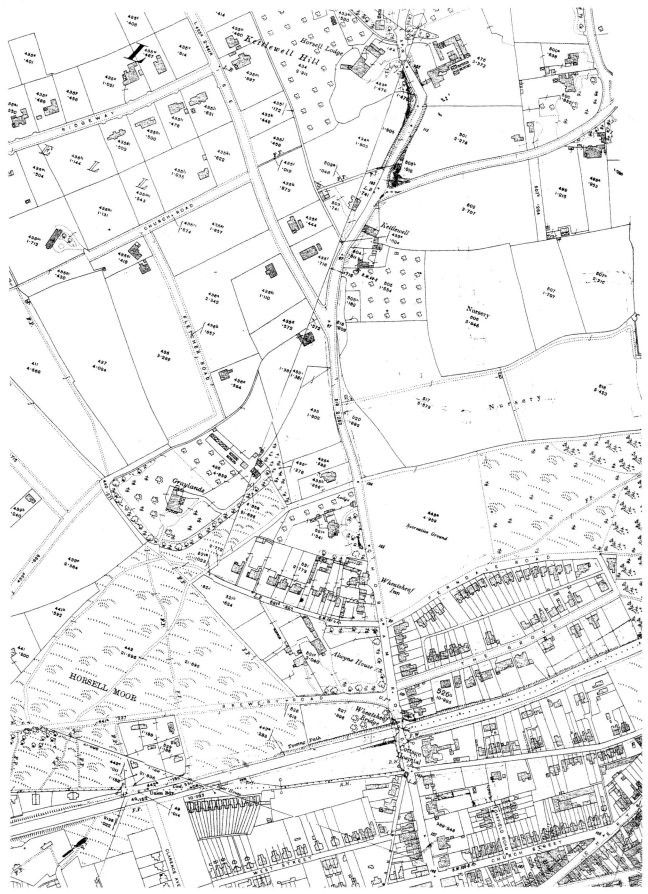

Figure 11(b) OS Map of the Wheatsheaf area in 1934

(Reproduced from the 1934 Ordnance Survey map; the scale of this copy is 1 inch represents about 120 yards.)

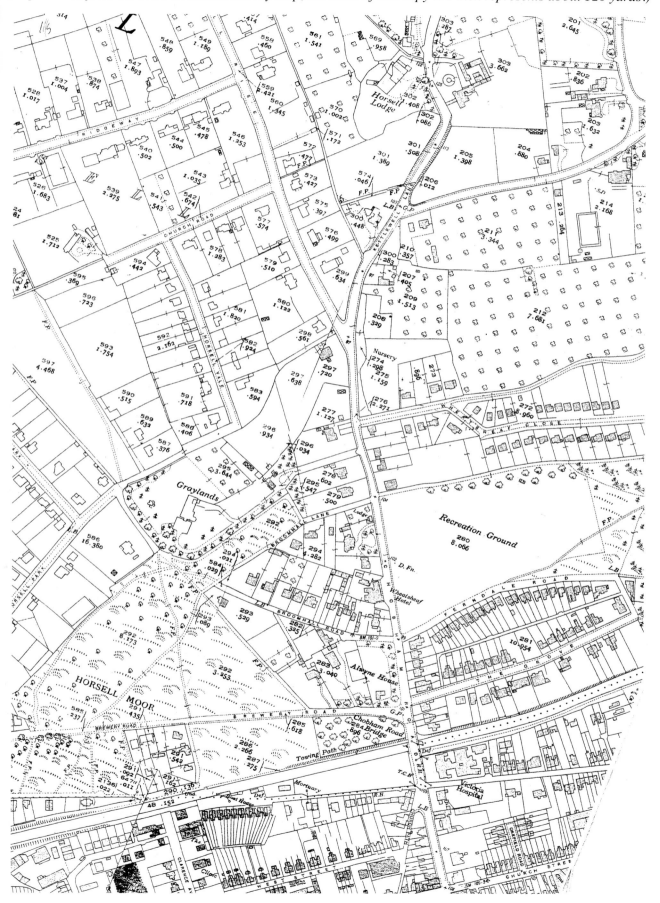

but by 1934 most plots had been built on. The only new roads on the 1934 map, Figure 11(b), are Broomhall Lane and Wheatsheaf Close; there had also been some building on Chobham road itself. Post-1934 the tributary roads, for greenfield development, were Orchard Drive, Horsell Park Close and Kettlewell Close. Thereafter only small corners of undeveloped land, or land being redeveloped, was available for further building. For this reason many small cul de sacs have been built usually containing three to a dozen dwellings. An exception to this fairly small scale development occurred at the top of Kettlewell Hill alongside Kettlewell Lane. There the site of a former gentleman's residence and grounds were large enough to accommodate 40 executive style detached houses. The grounds had not previously been developed because the residence had become a hospital annex with the grounds preserved.

Apart from developing or redeveloping land the other way the number of dwellings might increase was through the subdivision and/or extension of existing dwellings. This was the fate of several of the gentlemen's residences; but it also took place with smaller, but still sizeable, houses – particularly those near the Wheatsheaf Bridge and, therefore, in easy walking distance of the town and railway station.

5.2   Social changes

After the First World War there were substantial changes. For example Kelly's 1920s' Directories list several houses on Chobham Road as having 'apartments'; this was a short-lived phenomena for these entries had disappeared by the 1930s. However it is the changes to the gentlemen's residences that provide a striking insight on development trends. Nearly all these big houses, built over fifty years previously, sold off some of their grounds in the 1920s or 1930s. The houses themselves generally remained as private residences – sometimes subdivided. The first big house to change, perhaps because of its lack of privacy as the road outside became busier, was Broom Hall. In Kelly's 1915 Directory no one is entered as residing at Broom Hall while directories for the 1920s show it as housing Government Offices including a 'surveyor of taxes' and an 'old age pensions officer'. Land was sold in the 1920s for building but by 1930 the house had reverted to residential use but with the indignity of being subdivided – as it still is. Alwyne House and its extensive grounds remained intact until the last of the Compton family died in 1927. Then the estate was auctioned in six lots – four were potential building plots; the other two were Alwyne House and Alwyne Cottage which both remained as private houses with much reduced grounds until the 1960s. At Horsell Grange the big house was subdivided in the 1930s into three after the surrounding land had been sold. A different kind of redevelopment took place among the old cottages on The Wharf. The 1934 OS map shows several changes in the shape and position of the footprints of the dwellings as some of the old cottages were replaced by houses.

Thus, between the wars, redevelopment of existing properties took place at the same time as greenfield building. The latter was, numerically, the more important. An example previously studied (Harington 2004) is the development of what was advertised at the time as the Wheatsheaf Close Estate. This consisted of about fifty 3 or 4 bedroom detached houses on land that had been part of Vale Farm. The logistics had similarities to that of the Grove and Ferndale Road development at the turn of the century. Again a single developer was responsible and again the developer opted to use the word 'Wheatsheaf' – although the site had no direct connection with the original Wheatsheaf House.

Another inter-war change was the transformation of the old Wheatsheaf Inn into the new Wheatsheaf Hotel. This involved a complete rebuilding and realignment, probably involving the demolition of at least one old cottage.

A 19th Century feature that continued well into the 20th Century was the presence of a school. Section 3.5 mentioned the 19th Century school and also the one to be found in the 1901 Census with its four spinster schoolteachers. The same address was listed in Kelly's Directories for 1915 and 1919 as a 'preparatory school' – but the proprietor was a male with an M.A. degree; in the 1921 and 1922 Street Directories there was a different headmaster and it was now a 'preparatory school for boys'. However by 1923 the house was vacant and when once again occupied had reverted to a private address. The next mention of a school comes in the 1935 Directory with St Michael's Preparatory School and a Miss D Willis. However Miss Willis had been first listed at St Michael's in the 1926-27 Directory so possibly there had been a small school from that date. The school continued until 1939 but in the first post-war Directory had become a Day Nursery – and today is a Family Centre.

Another small scale enterprise was a Nursing Home that operated in two adjoining houses in The Grove for most of the interwar years. Then a 'Ladies' Association for Preventative & Rescue Work' (Kelly's Directory for 1915) was housed in Ferndale Road). This underwent several tactful changes of name until in the 1969 Street Directory it had become 'St Margaret's Home – Woking Deanery Association for Social Work'. For most of its existence this organisation occupied two houses.

Following the Second World War greenfield development continued – this included Orchard Drive (started before the War) and Horsell Park Close. Kettlewell Close was built on land sold off by Horsell Lodge. After this little open land remained and subsequent building was either infilling or redevelopment. Several of the big 19th Century residences were demolished and their sites built on. This was what happened to Alwyne House, to Alwyne Cottage and to Graylands (at the latter there had been no inter-war piecemeal sales of land – see Appendix 6 for details of the kind of 1930s' lifestyle that has been lost). At Graylands one dwelling was replaced by 92; perhaps the biggest single redevelopment ever in the area. When Kettlewell Hill House ceased to be a private residence it became an Annex to the local hospital but later was demolished and the land used for housing. This development (called Fairlawn) was the most recent, and possibly the last, large 'estate'. Nevertheless some gentlemen's residences, without much land, are still standing. Horsell Grange and Broomhall (both admittedly subdivided) have already been mentioned; and Horsell Lodge has been a residential home since the 1950s.

Demolition and redevelopment was also the fate of several houses with large gardens built in the 20th Century. For example today, along Chobham Road to the north of the old entrance to Graylands are Thurlton Court (12 town houses) and Laleham Court (42 apartments). These are both 1960s/1970s developments built on what were originally the grounds of two large early 20th Century houses. The former is of particular interest as Thurlton was the home of Dr Grantly Dick Read, the renowned advocate of natural childbirth, for most of the 1920s and 1930s (See Appendix 3 for more information). Smaller plots than Thurlton or Laleham could be combined for redevelopment. Thus one of the detached Victorian houses in Broomhall Road, together with the adjoining one-time builder's yard and a Victorian semi, have been replaced by a block of 16 flats. Another of these Victorian houses has been extended to more than twice its original size. (Thankfully, at present three still remain largely unchanged externally). On the other side of this road three large executive style detached houses have recently been built in garden of a 1930s' house – which itself had been built on a plot originally part of the Alwyne House grounds.

The greater density of housing in The Grove and Ferndale has meant that there has been little demolition and the changes have been mainly extensions or dividing large houses into flats or non-residential uses. This has also happened to the several houses on Chobham Road close to the town centre. Whereas the post-1930 detached houses in Wheatsheaf Close and Orchard Drive are little affected by redevelopment – apart from extensions. Their plots are too small, and the houses too valuable, to make redevelopment economic.

The frontispiece captures the late 1950s' situation in the southern part of the Wheatsheaf area. The Grove and Ferndale are much as they were when they were built; Alwyne House and Cottage are still standing; Brewery Road carpark is allotments and the Kingswood Court site is undeveloped.

Since 1985 the number of new dwellings has been, by historical standards, relatively small (Table 4). This is a reflection that there was little scope for greenfield building and even the redevelopment of large gardens is coming to an end. Demolishing one house to built two (or more) is still sometimes possible but has a limited effect. If high rise developments took place the number of dwellings might again accelerate. At present this is contrary to planning policy for the area.

5.3   Conclusion

Both the original development of the area after the coming of the railway, and all the subsequent redevelopments, provide an insight into many of the social changes that have taken place since 1840. The advantage of looking at a small area is that the details of individual people, of individual households, and individual buildings or pieces of land greatly add to the color, life and depth of the resulting picture.

Appendix 1

Key to Plot Numbers used on the 1851 Map (see Figure 2)

OWNERS.	OCCUPIERS.	No. on Plan.	DESCRIPTION.	STATE OF CULTIVATION.	QUANTITIES.		
			Brought Forward.		198	0	28
Stedman, Jas. Roake. &c.	Themselves,	92	Broomstile Lane		0	0	26
Roake, Henry,	Himself,	93	Broomstile Lane,		0	0	28
Roake, Henry,	Himself,	94	Sudrush,	Arable,	6	2	36
Stedman, James,	Himself,	95	Sudrush,	Arable,	4	0	16
Roake, Henry,	Himself	96	Church Field,	Arable,	21	0	39
Stedman, James,	Himself,	97	Broomstile Field,	Arable,	6	2	30
Stedman, James,	Himself,	98	Bessie Field,	Arable.	1	2	6
Suer, Richard,	Cobbett &c. Haron.,	99	Walldens Nursery	Arable.	5	1	31
Suer, Richard,	Cobbett &c. Haron.	100	House, Farm Gard. &c,	Nursery, &c,	2	1	6
Stedman, James,	Himself,	101	Malthouse, Homest., Brewery &c		1	0	10
Stedman, James,	Himself,	102	Home Field,	Arable,	8	0	25
Stedman, James,	Himself,	103	French Wheat Field,	Meadow,	3	0	11
Stedman, James,	Himself,	104	Ladderstile Field,	Meadow,	2	1	23
Stedman, James,	Himself	105	Black Mead,	Meadow,	2	3	34
Hammond, Wm.	Himself,	106	The Plat,	Meadow,	0	3	29
Cotton, Mr.,	Smith, Saml. &c.	107	Two Tenements & Gard.		0	3	22
Waterer, Jas. Trust. of	Haynes, James,	108	Cottage & Garden,		0	1	24
Waterer, Jas. Trust. of	Smith, Jas. Junr.	109	Cottage & Garden,		0	0	29
			Carried Forward,		272	2	13

From the previous page -

Whitburn, Sarah	Cobbett, James	86	Farm homestead & Garden	Arable	0	1	22
Whitburn, Sarah	Cobbett, James	87	Farm homestead & Garden	Arable	3	0	5
Whitburn, Sarah	Cobbett, James	88	Farm homestead & Garden	Arable	3	2	12
Whitburn, Sarah	Cobbett, James	89	Farm homestead & Garden	Arable	4	6	0
Whitburn, Sarah	Cobbett, James	90	Farm homestead & Garden	Arable	1	0	7
Daborn, James	Cobbett, James	91	Farm homestead & Garden	Arable	5	2	17

Note: The three columns of 'Quantities' are acres, roods, and square rods respectively. The first column is the most important in that it gives the area rounded down to the nearest whole acre; the formula to convert the columns to the exact area measured in acres is [column 1 + 0.25 (column 2) + 0.025 (column 3)]. One acre is 4840 square yards or 0.4047 hectares.

OWNERS.	OCCUPIERS.	No. on Plan.	DESCRIPTION.	STATE OF CULTIVATION.	QUANTITIES.		
			Brought Forward,		272	2	13
Hampton, Isaac,	Himself,	110	Cottage and Garden,		0	3	18
Cobbett, H. & Caroni.,	Themselves,	111	Storehouse,		0	0	1
Fletcher, Joseph,	Himself/Turner, Jas./	112	Ho. Schools, Chapel & Land,		2	1	30
Smither, Arthur,	Himself & others,	113	Three Houses & Gardens,		0	2	26
Smither, Arthur,	Percy, John,	114	Wheatsheaf Beer Ho. & Gar.,		0	0	27
Hayward David	Himself,	115	Cottage & Garden,		0	2	26
Common,	Common, /Waste/	116	Waste,		0	0	30
Stone, Henry,	Himself,	117	Cottage & Garden,		0	3	11
Whitburn, Sarah,	Cannon, Sarah,	118	Tenement & Garden,		0	0	39
Whitburn, Sarah,	Stone, John,	119	Tenement & Garden,		0	0	14
Whitburn, Sarah,	Cobbett, James,	120	Wheatsheaf Mead,	Meadow,	3	1	14
Fenn, John,	Fenn, Olive,	121	Pond Field,	Arable,	5	2	39
Fenn, John,	Fenn, Olive,	122	Heathy Field	Arable,	5	2	17
Roake, Henry,	Himself,	123	Little Shipley,	Arable,	4	1	1
Fenn, John,	Fenn, Olive,	124	Orchard Field,	Arable,	3	3	12
Fenn, John,	Fenn, Olive,	125	Farm Homestead & Orch.,	Meadow, &c,	2	0	26
Roake, Henry,	Himself,	126	Great Shipley,	Arable,	11	3	17
Roake, Henry,	Himself,	127	Nettewell Farm, Homest.,		1	2	15
			Carried Forward		317	0	14

From later pages -

Fenn, John	Fenn, Olive	136	Lower Shipley	Arable	3	1	23
	Public Road	648	On Common	Waste	1	0	34
	Waste	649	Common	Waste	19	0	20
	Public Road	650	On Common	Waste	0	2	34
	Waste	651	Common	Waste	0	1	14
	Waste	652	Common	Waste	5	2	28
	Waste	653	Common	Waste	44	0	28

An explanation of the three 'Quantities' columns is given on the first page of this Appendix.

Appendix 2

Key to Plot Numbers used on the 1871 OS map – Figure 7(a)

The key reproduced below is copied from the Parish Area Book. Horsell's Book is held at the British Library who kindly supplied this copy.

PARISH OF HORSELL. 5

No. on Plan.	Area in Acres.	Description.	No. on Plan.	Area in Acres.	Description.
390	2·320	Pasture.	442	2·951	Pasture.
391	10·465	Arable.	443	747·698	Rough pasture.
392	1·796	Arable.	443a	·300	Garden.
393	1·289	Arable.	444	·167	Towing path.
394	3·116	Pasture, &c.	445	1·158	Houses, gardens, &c.
395	1·000	Houses, gardens, &c.	446	3·130	Houses & gardens.
396	7·777	Nursery.	447	3·601	Houses, gardens, &c.
397	3·515	Arable.	448	·348	Private road.
398	1·091	Arable.	449	4·847	Arable.
399	1·947	Houses, sheds, garden, &c.	450	·332	House, garden, &c.
			451	2·695	Houses, gardens, &c.
400	2·141	Arable.	452	1·561	Houses, gardens, &c.
401	·971	Houses, gardens, &c.	453	3·212	Pasture.
402	·834	Church & graveyard.	454	1·097	Arable.
403	·571	House, garden, &c.	455	5·579	Arable.
404	2·451	Pasture, &c.	456	·246	Water.
405	3·569	Arable.	457	1·716	Pasture, &c.
406	1·366	Houses, gardens, &c.	458	3·846	Arable.
407	2·814	Arable.	459	5·428	Arable.
408	·816	Pasture.	460	3·371	Arable, &c.
409	1·675	Arable.	461	4·212	Arable.
410	1·228	Arable.	462	·560	House, garden, &c.
411	21·857	Arable, &c.	463	·867	House, garden, &c.
412	18·759	Arable, &c.	464	3·765	Public road.
413	1·847	Pasture, &c.	465	1·332	Farmsteading, &c.
414	6·102	Arable.	466	11·781	Arable, &c.
415	3·061	Arable.	467	6·781	Arable, &c.
416	·711	Private road.	468	21·020	Arable.
417	2·789	Pasture.	469	1·627	Houses, garden, &c.
418	1·296	Arable.	470	4·960	Arable.
419	3·519	Arable.	471	2·167	Arable.
420	3·761	Arable.	472	1·100	Arable.
421	1·274	Rough pasture.	473	·222	Private road.
422	·895	Pasture.	474	6·520	Pasture, &c.
423	1·982	Pasture.	475	1·949	Public road.
424	2·785	Public road.	476	11·614	Arable.
425	·651	Houses, gardens, &c.	477	·511	Private road.
426	3·246	Houses, gardens, &c.	478	2·699	Arable.
427	10·656	Arable.	479	2·052	House, sheds, garden, &c.
428	6·180	Arable.			
429	1·098	Arable, &c.	480	4·827	Arable, &c.
430	1·714	Houses, gardens, &c.	481	·778	Farmsteading, &c.
431	5·221	Arable.	482	21·784	Arable.
432	7·670	Arable, &c.	483	9·073	Arable.
433	7·565	Arable, &c.	484	6·900	Arable.
434	6·713	Arable, &c.	485	2·244	Arable.
435	27·386	Arable, &c.	486	1·976	Arable.
436	6·928	Arable.	487	·240	Water.
437	4·024	Arable.	488	5·318	Water (canal).
438	5·579	Arable.	489	·470	Rough pasture, &c.
439	22·153	Arable.	490	·131	Water.
440	·230	Rough pasture.	491	2·625	Arable.
441	1·486	Houses & gardens.	492	5·062	Public road.

Appendix 3

Thurlton and Dr Grantly Dick Read

Thurlton was a large house on Chobham Road on the Kettlewell side of the entrance to Graylands; today 12 town houses (Thurlton Court) occupy the site. On the 1912 OS map, Figure 11(a), there is no building on the plot (numbered 435) but there is one on the 1934 OS map; the first Street Directory that includes the house is 1924's and the occupant is given as Dr Grantly Dick Read. This seems to indicate the house was built in the early 1920s; Dr Read's biography (Noyes Thomas 1957) gives no details. It is however stated that the move to Woking in 1923 was 'a bitter blow' made because Mrs Read insisted on a move out of London. There was soon a clinic in Woking followed by one in Harley Street. Dr Read lived at Thurlton for over 20 years. He went to South Africa in 1948 – frustrated by the medical establishment and wanting to make a fresh start for personal reasons. It was at Thurlton that Dr Read did most of the writing about natural childbirth that made him famous.

In its account of some domestic crises in the Second World War the biography gives some information about the property. When war broke out Dr Read was on holiday with his family. They returned to find evacuees had already been assigned to them. One family had been allocated the billiard room; in another context there is mention of 'the library'. So the indications are that it was a large house. In the grounds there were evidently two cottages at the bottom of the back garden and a lodge 'at the bottom of the drive'. (The biography mentioned the former because they were hit by a war time bomb and the latter because 'the little place' was offered as accommodation to close friends.)

According to the biography Dr Read and his family lived at Thurlton throughout the war; as apparently did a number of evacuees about whom Dr Read wrote in an exasperated tone 'I become irritable with the children, the dogs, the chickens and the women'. There seem to have been other occupants as well for the Fire Guard register (SHC 6650/1) has several volunteers from the Ministry of Supply (Department of Home Grown Timber) giving the Thurlton as their address. After Dr Read had left, the 1950 Street Directory listed 'Forestry Commission, S.E. Area' as the sole occupants; however by time of the next Directory (1957) it had reverted to a private house. The site was redeveloped in the 1960s.

Appendix 4

Kettlewell and Kettlewell House – some complications

The mid-nineteenth century censuses consistently recorded three properties on the ridge of higher ground at Kettlewell. At the foot of the south facing slope were two farmhouses; both are on the 1851 and 1871 maps and can be identified in the censuses. The third, larger, property was on the top of the ridge – usually two dwellings were recorded there. One, Kettlewell House, was listed in 1841, 1851 and 1861; but not 1871 when it may have been uninhabited. The second dwelling was not named in 1841, was Kettlewell Farm in 1851 (with an agricultural labourer as household head), and was Kettlewell Cottage in 1861 and 1871. That the combination of Kettlewell Farm and Kettlewell Cottage did not occur in any census may mean there was a working farm – but not the usual farmhouse and farmer. Instead there was a residence with a gentleman farmer and a dwelling for his foreman or bailiff. Different census enumerators gave the dwellings different names.

It is outside the scope of this paper to give a history of Kettlewell House. What follows is limited to the information used in trying to deduce what happened to the site from 1841 onwards:

(a) Two 18th Century Wills are relevant. One is that of (463) 'Henry Roake of Kettlewell, gentleman' (died 1756) and the other (488) of 'Richard Roake of Kettlewell, gentleman' (died 1769). These Wills show that both men had owned several pieces of land in the Woking/Chertsey/Chobham area. Neither will mentions Kettlewell House or Farm but the phrase '… of Kettlewell, gentleman' is a pointer to a residence.

(b) The Land Tax records for around 1790-1800 include 'Richard Roake of Kettlewell' (again without specifying House or Farm) paying an amount of tax that indicates he was a big land owner – regrettably the accompanying description is merely 'House and Land'. The records for 1810-1830 also include 'Richard Roake' but this time without mentioning Kettlewell. Presumably this was the Richard Roake who was included in the parish burial records for 1838 aged 70. Following this death, the Land Tax entries for 1839-1844 refer to a Henry Roake – probably a son. But in 1845 although Henry Roake was again listed the amount of tax was greatly reduced. His link with Kettlewell may have been broken.

(c) The 1834 Parish Survey did not mention Kettlewell House or Kettlewell Farm although other houses and farms were named. Yet a field, known from other records to adjoin Kettlewell Farm, was listed as being owned and occupied (i.e. farmed) by a Richard Roake. He was also shown as the occupier/owner of a 'House, Garden and Rickyard'; again the location of this house was not stated and he was given as the owner/occupier of several other houses.

(d) The 1841 Census included Kettlewell House but the occupants were given, improbably for a gentleman's residence, as a farmer and his family. In 1851 this same farmer was listed at another, smaller, farm in the Kettlewell area; and, in 1861, when he had retired he lived in a labourer's cottage – so seems unlikely ever to have been a gentleman farmer. However in 1841 another unnamed dwelling a family was enumerated who were much more plausible occupants of a gentleman's residence – a 45-year-old man on half pay from the army, his daughter, and two servants. A possible explanation of this anomaly is that the enumerator mixed up the house descriptions. (There was no mention of a member of the Roake family in 1841 despite Henry Roake's inclusion in the Land Tax records.)

(e) Ryde's 1851 map shows one sizeable dwelling and one small dwelling together with many farm buildings. Neither dwelling was named or numbered but the complex has the word 'KETTLEWELL' written beside it. This suggests that the identifier of 'House' or 'Farm' was not of primary importance; both were just part of 'Kettlewell'. Surprisingly Ryde's key to the map did not mention Kettlewell House but did include Kettlewell Farm (as can be seen in Appendix 1). The farm's owner occupier was given as Henry Roake with a dwelling occupying a plot of 1.6 acres – he was also listed as the owner of a lot of farmland. (His inclusion is strange in that he was not enumerated in the 1841 Census and the Land Tax records suggest the possibility that he left Kettlewell in the mid-1840s – see above.)

(f)   In the 1851 and 1861 Censuses the dwelling definitely was a gentleman's residence. For in 1851 the householder was absent but a housekeeper, a groom and a visitor were recorded. In 1861 there was a businessman's household.

(g)   The 1871 OS map, like the 1851 map, names Kettlewell Farm but not Kettlewell House. Both maps also show a footpath leading almost from the front door of the larger dwelling towards Horsell village (part of it still exists). This footpath is very straight which suggests it is old which, in turn, is in keeping with the Kettlewell complex of buildings being old.

(h)   The 1871 Census lists Kettlewell Cottage with the household head's occupation as 'Bailiff Kettlewell Farm'. This Census lists neither the Farm nor Kettlewell House. However there was an uninhabited, and so unnamed, dwelling which was probably one or the other.

(i)   The 1881 and 1891 Censuses included The Grange but not Kettlewell House or Farm. In 1881 there was a Grange Cottage occupied by a 'Farm Bailiff'; in 1891 there was no such cottage.

(j)   The 1896 OS map shows Horsell Grange on the site of what, on the 1871 OS map, had been Kettlewell Farm. The footprint of the buildings is different in that what had been separate buildings in 1871 were continuous in 1896; and the large field around the farm had been subdivided into building plots. (The redevelopment may be why in 1871 there was an uninhabited dwelling. Section 4.7 mentions sales of land from the Horsell Grange Estate).

(k)   None of the nineteenth century Kelly's Directories included Kettlewell House. Kettlewell Farm occurred in two – 1874 and 1882. The Grange (or Horsell Grange) first appeared in 1882 and regularly thereafter. What may be significant is that in 1882 it was the same person who had The Grange as a private address and, under the business entries, was shown as a farmer at Kettlewell Farm. In the next Directory (for 1887) this individual had The Grange as a private address and was also listed as a farmer at The Grange – with no mention of Kettlewell Farm.

(l)   The 1901 Census did list Kettlewell House but this may not have been the same building as that recorded in earlier censuses. Moreover the word 'House' soon disappeared. The 1901 Census occupant appears in the 1899 and 1903 Kelly's Directory with the address of simply 'Kettlewell'. This address continued to feature in subsequent directories.

(m)   The earliest Street Directory is one for 1921. This, unlike Kelly's, lists every house and includes Kettlewell as the name of a dwelling – but not Kettlewell House. Kettlewell continued to appear until the 1964 Street Directory. Planning maps show that this house stood on land which had been fields on the 1896 OS map.

There is a print dated 1824 of 'Old Kettlewell House' (SHC 4348/3/98/3). It shows a substantial, but plain, dwelling in open parkland. The actual setting of the House was close to a road but at the time such visual spin was an accepted convention. The present house looks nothing like the house in the print because of the 1870s' makeover of Kettlewell House into Horsell Grange. This gave the house an early Georgian style exterior. Crosby reproduced the print and describes the house as 'an attractive 18th century building with large grounds, was demolished in the 1930s and its land used for superior housing'. There is a misunderstanding here. What happened in the 1930s was that Horsell Grange was bought by a local builder/developer. He converted the house into three apartments and sold some of the grounds around it for building (and one of these new houses was named 'Horsell Grange'). This was the culmination of the selling off of Horsell Grange land that had begun in the late 19th Century.

To sum up, Kettlewell is an old settlement and there was a residence there long before the coming of the railway (or the canal). Probably originally 'Kettlewell' was an adequate address without a distinction between House, Farm and Cottage. When these terms were used there were inconsistencies over time. The farm ceased to operate some time between 1880 and 1890 when the surrounding fields were sold for building; and at much the same time the existing buildings were much altered, extended, and rebranded as Horsell Grange. An unsolved mystery is why such a long established, and presumably important, house did not feature at all in the Parish Survey of 1834, in Ryde's Survey of 1851, on the 1871 OS map, and in the early Kelly's Directories.

Appendix 5

Alwyne House and the Compton family

Alwyne House was first listed in the 1861 Census; judging from the birthplaces of the children it was built in the late 1850s (see below). This was the first of the new gentlemen's residences – but was not built until about twenty years after the coming of the railway. Ryde's 1851 map shows earlier buildings on the site but these had been on a 2 acre property whereas Alwyne House had grounds of 5 acres.

Figure 12.   Alwyne House in the 1960s

Although showing signs of neglect the house had evidently been an imposing gentleman's residence. In its early years horse drawn carriages would swing round and pull up at the impressive entrance. The stables at the rear could be entered from Broomhall Road.

Details of occupants from the census returns (ages were not always consistent between censuses) are:

1861   Spencer Compton, aged 46. Occupation – Land, Fund, and Stockholder – born in Middlesex; and his wife Alicia, aged 40, born in Devon. There were 3 children – Anne aged 20 born in Devon, Alicia aged 6 and Charles aged 4. There was a 17-year-old General Servant. The younger children had been born in Peckham so the family must have moved to Horsell sometime after 1856/7 – and before 1859 as Horsell records show the burial of an 11-week-old Compton baby then.

1871   The same family but the son, Charles, was absent. (There is evidence that he was an invalid or handicapped; he died in 1882 aged 25.) Spencer Compton's occupation was given as 'East India Merchant'. There were two servants – a cook and a housemaid. There was a 'Gardeners Cottage' occupied by the gardener and his wife with a groom as a lodger. (This was the only census in which a servants' cottage was linked with Alwyne House.)

1881   The family members were unchanged, with two different servants. Spencer Compton was now 67 and entered as a 'retired East India Merchant'; he died later in the year. His personal estate was valued at £15,000 – a considerable sum.

1891   The widow and the older daughter were enumerated; the younger daughter was not. Once more there were two different servants.

1901   The widow, now 83, and the two daughters; again with two different servants.

The widow died towards the end of 1901, the younger daughter in 1922 and the older daughter in 1927 at about age 86 having lived in the house for 70 years. There is a Compton family gravestone in Horsell churchyard.

A Spencer Compton was listed from 1837 to 1866 in the Bombay Directory of the East India Company (held in the Oriental and India Office Collections of the British Library). He attained the rank of covenanted (senior) officer in the Bombay Civil Service from 1862 onwards. The British Library's index of bonds for Europeans travelling to India record a Charles Spencer Compton being given permission on 13th June 1833 to travel to Bengal via China. (*e-mails from Dorian Leveque* of Reference Services, Oriental and India office Collections.) At SHC there are documents (2593/1) regarding land in Shanghai purchased by a Charles Spencer Compton in the 1850s or 1860s; after his death in 1869 the Alwyne House daughters were mentioned in the winding up of Charles's estate. It seems beyond reasonable doubt that Charles Spencer Compton and Spencer Compton of Alwyne House were closely related – most probably brothers (remembering that Charles was the name of Spencer Compton's son).

When Alwyne House was built a second dwelling had been built in the grounds close by as can be seen from the frontispiece. This was Alwyne Cottage and the occupants in 1861 were three older, unmarried, sisters of Spencer Compton – with a servant. In 1871 and 1881 there were two sisters; in 1891 one sister aged 85. (For Spencer Compton to have had three unmarried sisters and then two daughters who never married must have been unusual even for that time.) By 1901 Alwyne Cottage was occupied by a different family – a young solicitor, his wife, two children and two servants.

After the death of the last Miss Compton in 1927 the estate was subdivided into 6 lots which were sold at auction. Alwyne House and Alwyne Cottage were sold, with much reduced grounds, and remained in residential use. The other four lots were of land suitable for building. The first to be developed was that alongside Chobham Road; on it, in the 1930s, four detached houses were built. In the mid 1960s Alwyne House was demolished and replaced by Trinity Methodist church while Alwyne Cottage stood until the early 1970s when it was demolished and replaced by flats.

Appendix 6

Graylands – the story of a gentleman's residence

This is the only 'gentleman's residence' for which detailed information has been obtained *(by a personal communication from Mrs Vera Namsoo)* about the appearance of the house and grounds when they were in their prime. The first census in which Graylands appeared was 1881's. Then it was listed as 'Greysend House' and judging from the sequence of addresses the enumerator had approached the house from Horsell Moor; whereas in both 1891 and 1901 it was listed as 'Graylands' and had been approached from Kettlewell Lane. This suggests that the house was very new in 1881.

Figure 13(a) Graylands – the house in 1935

Details of occupants from the census returns are:

1881   Joseph FitzGerald aged 45, Foreign Timber merchant – born in Lambeth, his wife Catherine aged 35 born in Sussex, four daughters (ages 9, 7, 6 and 3) all born in Horsell, and 3 servants. In 1871 Joseph had been enumerated, as an unmarried man living with his widowed mother, at the nearby Broom Hall.

1891   William Roebuck aged 62, Civil Engineer born in Yorkshire and his wife Eliza aged 41 born in Kent, no children, 5 servants; and 5 children of two of the servants who were a married couple. Possibly this couple and their children should have been recorded as being in a separate house – the husband was a coachman and there were stables and a cottage.

1901   William Walker aged 20, Contractors Clerk born in Middlesex, and 2 servants are the only occupants. William Walker is entered as 'grandson' in the Relation to Head of Family column but the Head was not enumerated. In Kelly's 1899 Directory it is Mrs Roebuck who is listed as the occupant at Graylands so presumably Mr. Roebuck had died. I have not established whether William Walker was Mrs Roebuck's grandson or whether a new family had moved in.

Figure 13(b)   Graylands – plan of the grounds

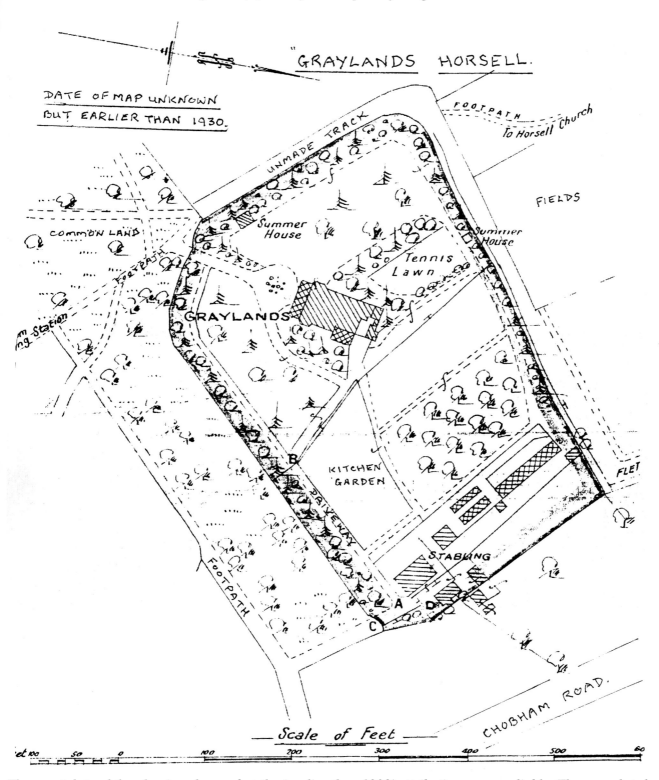

Scale of Feet

The exact date of the plan is unknown but the 'earlier than 1930' attribution seems reliable. The convoluted way in from Chobham Road is as marked on the 1912 OS map whereas the 1934 map has a more direct approach. Also 'FLET' on the right hand side is Fletcher Road – a name which was changed in the mid-thirties. Given that the map was supplied by a member of the Ferguson family the likelihood is that this was a plan dating from their purchase of Graylands. An incidental point of interest is that trees are now marked on the common land – which earlier had been treeless.

Comparing the 1871 and 1896 OS maps, Figures 7(a) and (b), Graylands was built on a field – plot 438 in Figure 7(a) – to which access was across a part of Horsell Moor. This presumably is why a rather devious route for carriages or vehicles had been devised to get onto Chobham Road – although the 1896 OS map shows that the Moor lying between Graylands and Chobham Road had been enclosed. Eventually more direct access across this land was obtained and is marked on 1934 OS map. The house was demolished in the 1960s but unusually the site was not then subdivided; part of the original garden wall is still standing. The person who kindly supplied the plan and the picture of the house reproduced in Figures 13 (a) & (b) also provided a pen-picture of Graylands (the words in italics are my interjections)-

'I lived at Graylands from 1935 *(the writer was then 18)* with my parents, Mr. & Mrs James Ferguson. Purchase price £3,500!

We were told that prior to Graylands a large farmhouse stood on the site and owned much of the surrounding area of that part of Horsell. When this was demolished Graylands was built on the same foundations. *(Illustrates how quickly legends take root! Figure 7(a) and the census returns show there was no such farmhouse).* A Mr. & Mrs Churchill owned it then, who were true gentry of their time owning ponies and traps … *(Kelly's Directories for 1911 and 1924 list Col. & Mrs Churchill; they are not in the 1909 or 1930 Directory).*

Graylands was really special … with its ¼ mile sweeping drive flanked by huge trees and rhododendron hedges, opening onto vast lawns with cedar and sweet chestnut trees and an orchard full of daffodils. There was also a huge kitchen garden and greenhouses.

The lovely old redbrick house stood in the centre of five acres. Semicircular stone steps led up to the heavy oak door with its Greek bronze knocker. The hall was panelled in oak and the oak staircase swept up three walls to six large bedrooms in the main part of the house. *(Some details of the contents follow.)*

The rear of the house was the servants' quarters opening onto a walled courtyard with various outhouses and a deep basement boiler house … There were large cellars beneath the front part of the house…

In 1961 Mr. Ferguson decided to retire. Being unable to sell the house as it stood, and as an adjoining property was being demolished to build a block of flats, he drew up plans to develop Graylands as a luxury development while retaining the fine lawn and trees. The plan was passed by the then housing minister, Sir Keith Joseph, to erect three separate blocks of three storey apartments, one on the house site, one in the orchard, and one where the stable stood. There would be an underground garage area in the far corner with a children's enclosed playground above. The lawns would remain as communal gardens with their shrubbery borders. But unfortunately he died before his dream could be reality and the development company who purchased the site had other ideas.' *(There are now five separate, three storey, blocks of apartments, with some communal open space, on the site. Some of the original boundary garden walls remain as well as the direct drive – in from Chobham Road – now a footpath.)*

Bibliography

The main sources for analysing the trends in the number of households and people and their characteristics are, of course, the ten-yearly Censuses of Population from 1841 to 1901. Maps add a more precise geographical dimension but are only available at irregular intervals:

Parish Survey of 1851 by Edward Ryde. The first map that can be related to a census is a large-scale map (SHC 6198/11/188) of Horsell Parish for 1851; part of it is shown in Figure 2. Every piece of land, including every dwelling, is numbered and an accompanying Book of Reference (SHC 6198/11/189) gives the owner, the occupier/tenant, a description of the land use, the state of cultivation (for fields), and the physical size. The survey was carried out by the Order of the Board of Guardians of the Chertsey Union, within whose ambit Horsell parish lay, with the work being done by Edward Ryde. Nearly all the occupiers of dwellings were enumerated in the 1851 Census so that that Census can be mapped. This then helps with other censuses.

Ordnance Survey Maps for 1871, 1896, 1912 and 1934. These are the dates of the large-scale (25 inches to the mile) OS maps. Each dwelling is marked but only the largest are named. For 1871 there are Parish Area Books which give similar information to the Book of Reference for 1851 but without the name of the owner or occupier.

Other sources include -

Parish Survey of 1834. (SHC 2283/7/1). This has a listing giving similar information to Edward Ryde's 1851 Book of Reference but without a map.

Land Tax records. (SHC 2283/6/7) These are available for 1781-1832 and for 1839-1878. The annual summary has four columns – Proprietor, Occupier, Description, and Sum Assessed. The descriptions are entries like 'House and Land' or 'Cottages and Gardens'; only rarely is there an indication of location. The Assessment varies from a few shillings to, exceptionally, about £15; the amounts are usually the same each year.

Kelly's Directory of Surrey. The earliest is for 1855 – followed by those for 1867, 1874, 1882, 1887 and then at intervals varying between one and four years until 1938. They list for Horsell parish, in alphabetical order of surnames with an address, those residents who agreed to their names being included (the early directories are more selective than the later ones). Copies are held at SHC.

Woking Year Book and Directory. The earliest is for 1921. Then they are annual until 1938. After the Second World War they are available for 1948 and 1949 but then only intermittently until 1969. They list every house in every street with the name of the head of household. Usually the order of the listing is actual sequence of the houses along each side of the street. Sometimes the two sides are combined so it is not clear what the sequence was on the ground or on which side of the street a particular house stood. Copies are held at SHC.

Some other primary sources are referred to in the text. The books cited are:

Crosby, A. (2003) *A History of Woking,* Chichester, Phillimore
Harington, A. (2004) *A History of Wheatsheaf Close,* unpublished
Horn, P. (1995) *The Rise and Fall of the Victorian Servant,* Stroud, Sutton
Noyes Thomas, A. (1957) *Doctor Courageous,* London, Heinemann
Victoria County History of Surrey, 1911 Edition, Vol. 3
Wilson, A. N. (2002) *The Victorians,* London, Hutchinson